Ines Scheurmann

Aquarium Fish Breeding

Breeding Instructions for
Cichlids, Characins, Catfish, and
other Popular Fish

With Color Photographs by Well-Known Photographers
and Drawings by Fritz W. Köhler

Consulting Editor: Matthew M. Vriends, Ph.D.

BARRON'S

Cover Photos
Front cover: Paradise fish pair under foam nest.
Inside front cover: Discus (*Symphysodon)* is
surrounded by its brood.
Inside back cover: Mouth-breeding cichlid female
(*Pseudotropheus zebra* "bright blue")
with brood in mouth.
Back cover: Mouth-breeding cichlids (*Geophagus
surinamensis*) with brood.

English translation © Copyright 1990
by Barron's Educational Series, Inc.

© Copyright 1989 by Gräfe and Unzer
GmbH, Munich, West Germany
The title of the German book is
Aquarienfische züchten

Translated from the German by
Arthur Freud and Rauel E. Ugarte

All inquiries should be addressed to:
Barron's Educational Series, Inc.
250 Wireless Boulevard
Hauppauge, NY 11788
Library of Congress Catalog Card No. 90-1005
International Standard Book No. 0-18120-4474-6
Library of Congress Cataloging-in-Publication Data
Scheurmann, Ines, 1950-
(Aquarienfische züchten. English)
Aquarium fish breeding : instructions for breeding
cichlids, characins, catfish, and other popular fish Ines
Scheurmann ; with color photographs by well-known
photographers and drawings by Fritz W. Köhler :
(translated from the German by Arthur Freud and
Rauel E. Ugarte).
Translation of: Aquarienfische züchten.
Includes bibliographical references and index.
ISBN 0-8120-4474-6
1. Aquarium fishes — Breeding. I. Title.
SF457.9.S3413 1990   90-1005
639.3'4 — dc20   CIP
PRINTED AND BOUND IN HONG KONG
2   4900   98765432

Photo Credits:
Elias: Pages 9, 55, 74, 101, 119; Hieronimus/Geobios:
page 84; Kahl: front cover; Kammereit: inside back
cover; Meulengracht-Madsen/Biophoto: inside front
cover, pages 20, 56; Schmidt/Geobios: pages 10, 73,
102 bottom, 120; Seegers: pages 37, 38; Sommer:
page 19; Werner/Geobios; page 83, back cover;
Zurlo: page 102 top.

About the Author:
Ines Scheurmann studied biology, specializing in the
behavior of fish, and has had many years of practical
experience in the care and breeding of aquarium fish.
She is the author of the Barron's pet owner's manual
Water Plants in the Aquarium and of Barron's *The
New Aquarium Fish Handbook*.

A Note of Warning:
In this book electrical equipment for the maintenance
of aquariums is described. Please be sure to observe
the instructions on page 13; otherwise serious
accidents may occur. Before buying a large aquarium,
check how much weight the floor can support in the
location where you will set up the aquarium
(see page 13).
It is not always possible to avoid water damage
resulting from broken glass, overflow or leaks that
develop in the tank. Therefore, be sure to obtain
insurance against such accidents. This can generally
be part of your homeowners or other liability policy.
Watch out that children (or adults) do not eat
aquarium plants. This could cause serious health
problems. Also, keep all fish medications, disinfectants, and other chemicals out of reach of children.

Contents

Foreword

The successful breeding of aquarium fish is the "masterpiece" of the aquarium hobbyist, and many hobbyists would like to achieve this success. You too can become a successful breeder if you understand the two basic requirements. First, you must acquire detailed knowledge about the behavior of each species of fish that you would like to breed. This will be your apprenticeship work. Second, you must be aware that many fish in the aquarium will reproduce only if given special living conditions that approximate those of their native habitat. You should therefore know more about your fish than the average hobbyist. This book contains the specialized knowledge that makes a master out of an apprentice.

Using precise terminology, Ines Scheurmann gives practical advice for the breeding of cichlids, characins, catfish and other popular fish. She includes suggestions that even the novice will find easy to follow. The breeding instructions have special sections about the selection of fish, construction and equipment of breeding tanks, reproductive behavior, egg handling, rearing of the fry, and important information about the water conditions, a critical feature that often spells the difference between success and failure.

In addition to the individual breeding instructions, in which the long years of experience of the author and several other experts come into play, this book also imparts a general knowledge of fish breeding that will help the beginner to avoid errors right from the start. This includes information about the water conditions in breeding and maintenance tanks. It is true that you can keep fish for years under water conditions which are merely adequate. But without ideal water conditions, you cannot motivate them to breed. A separate chapter about water will help you to overcome this ticklish problem.

The feeding of fish and fry is another important subject that can spell the difference between breeding success or failure. Many fish can be stimulated to breed only when they are fed for a lengthy period with live food. You will learn about individual feeding requirements in the detailed chapter on feeding.

The behavior patterns of the various species of fish also play an important role in successful breeding. You must know these so that you can create living conditions for your fish that are tailored to their reproductive requirements. For example, many fish will breed only when you simulate the conditions of the rainy season in their native habitat. The author provides many tested breeding suggestions. She also describes many other behavioral traits and explains exactly what you can do to stimulate breeding. In this way the fascinating behavioral mosaic of the fish is revealed. There are fish that, prior to spawning, polish stones until they are smooth; others build spawning nests; many form lasting partnerships, while others come together only for mating. You will find fish that move their fins to aerate the water for their eggs and fish that solicitously suck their young from the eggshell. But you will also find fish that do not care for their eggs or young, and even eat them.

Many of these absorbing behavioral patterns are pictured in this book in brilliant, unusually lifelike photos and informative illustrations.

With its sound suggestions and precise breeding instructions, this book is a reliable companion to successful breeding and provides a storehouse of information for every aquarium hobbyist who wants to do more.

About Breeding Fish

The breeding of fish is the most interesting, and the most difficult task that the aquarium hobbyist can undertake. Only by recreating the living conditions found in the wild can the aquarist encourage the fish to behave just as they would in their natural habitat and ultimately to breed. If you manage to induce your fish to bring forth young, you will enjoy the greatest feeling of success the aquarium hobbyist can ever have.

From Hobbyist to Amateur Breeder

Hobbyists who rejoice over their first accidental success with breeding live bearers such as toothed carp, rainbow fish, or some other relatively undemanding species are still not experienced breeders. Curiosity, a love of nature, and interest in strange forms of life are, along with endless patience, conscientiousness, and perseverance, the basic prerequisites for success with the more demanding breeds such as barbs and characins.
• Enjoying new knowledge. Whether you are interested in the fundamentals of heredity, the most recent aquarial technology, the chemical reactions of water, or the special needs of a specific fish species—the more thoroughly you study the material, the more easily you will understand complicated relationships and resolve breeding problems.
• Observation and care. Take as much time as possible to observe your fish. Observation creates a capacity for sympathy, and the combination of sympathy and knowledge provide the vital instincts for breeding many kinds of fish.
• Skills in aquarial technique and chemistry.
• Room for several tanks. In addition to a community tank, you will need at least one or more additional breeding and rearing tanks.

Sources of Information
• Specialized literature will be your first step in solving special problems (see the list of books on page 133.
• In addition, every large city, and even in the smaller towns, have aquarium clubs where the newcomer can get advice and help from more experienced aquarium hobbyists.
• Those with an interest in the behavior, care, and breeding of specific fish can join one of the national or international societies devoted to specific groups. There is a cichlid society, a killifish society, and many others (see addresses, page 133).

What Distinguishes the Amateur from the professional breeder?
If you imagine that you will make a lot of money from breeding aquarium fish you would be well advised not to start. Painstakingly bred fish, like all domestic animals, entail greater expenses than profits. The reward for effort, work, and the expense of fish breeding is in the excitement, fun, and skills you will develop. In addition, there is the joy of achieving success and the feeling of having contributed a small bit to the preservation of a species.

Amateur breeders maintain and breed fish differently from the professional. Professional breeders have to produce as many young as possible in order to make a profit. They maintain large numbers of fish under highly unnatural conditions in aquariums containing only the barest necessities for breeding. In breeding, feeding and the care of the brood, they take pragmatic measures that the amateur breeder would never consider because of space and costs.

What is important to amateurs is not the number of fish but their well-being and the enjoyment of their behavior during spawning and breeding. Aquarium hobbyists will try to provide not only the appropriate water conditions for breeding, but will do their best to approximate the environmental conditions under which the animals lived in their natural habitat so that the fish can engage in their most natural behavior.

Hobbyists will not tolerate empty aquariums except when unavoidable for hygienic reasons or for the care of sensitive species. They will return the fish as soon as possible to fully equipped aquariums.

About Breeding Fish

Tropical Fish Breeding and Protection of the Species

Not all aquarists are aware of the fact that nearly all fish species are regularly imported from their native habitat. Unlike the aviculturists, aquarists have up to now made hardly any effort to preserve rare and endangered tropical fish species through aquarium breeding.

A Special Species of Cavebreeders: In Lake Tanganyika there are many types of cichlids that spawn in empty snail shells and care there for their brood. In *Lamprologus boulengeri* the female alone cares for the eggs, while the larger male defends the territory.

In 1987 heated discussions broke out over laws promulgated by German authorities for wildlife protection that completely prohibited the importa-tion of certain coral fish species. The aquarist groups were at a disadvantage because they could not provide evidence of activities to protect fish. As a result of these discussions, a few self-evident rules for responsible behavior on the part of aquarium hobbyists are presented:
• If you acquire a rare species of tropical fish, you must apply your knowledge to do whatever is necessary to breed this species.
• Keep abreast of the available scientific literature dealing with the habits of this species. If you lack access to such literature, you will be able to find friends in aquarists' clubs who will have access to such material.
• The exchange of information—and of fish— between hobbyists is indispensable for the perpetuation of a species in the aquarium. You can avoid losses and the pitfalls of inbreeding by such exchanges. Thus it is important to start out with a sufficiently large breeding population.
• Avoid crossbreeding between populations (see page 8) of the same species with different genetic backgrounds.

What are Species, Subspecies, and Populations?

Species originate during the course of evolution through the adaptation of living forms to their environment; thus they are not unchangeable units. The climate, water composition, food supply, danger from predators, and so on change very slowly but persistently over time, and living things must adjust to minute changes in the environment from generation to generation. All environmental factors have an effect upon the characteristics of living things, in that changes in the environment bring about changes of behavior and even changes in bone and organ structure. Animals of one species do not crossbreed with those of other species, since fertile descendants are obtained only through propagation with members of the same species.

Subspecies are smaller subunits of a species. Subspecies are common among animals that are spread over wide areas with very different environments, as, for example, carp from Europe and northern Asia. Since inhabitants of the same area are formed by the same environmental conditions, they resemble each other but differ sharply in appearance and behavior from members of the same species in other environments.

About Breeding Fish

Populations are reproductive communities within a species or subspecies. At any given time they include the inhabitants of a limited environment that come into contact with each other and bring forth offspring. For example, different populations of *Tropheus mooru* live on the rocky shores Lake Tanganyika.

Populations living in areas widely separated from each other can, as a result of different environmental conditions, develop different patterns of behavior. Even mating and reproductive behavior can change within a species. Thus, the fish will have an affinity only toward members of their own population.

Populations can resemble each other in bone structure, teeth, and the shape of their fins and scales, and still have developed different behavior patterns. If fish populations are intermingled during importation, the aquarium hobbyist may acquire animals with different forms of breeding behavior which may be incompatible in mating and rearing of the young.

Crossbreeding in the Aquarium

Different species of fish almost never crossbreed in the wild. This is true even of closely related species. An exception to this is the carp, which is often referred to as the bastard species of the wild. The offspring of crossbreeding are almost always sterile (incapable of reproducing) and thus they cannot propagate the heritage of their parents. Nature has erected several barriers to crossbreeding:

• Eggs prefer sperm of the same species. When eggs come into contact with a sperm mixture in which sperm of a different species predominate, they will be preferentially fertilized by sperm of the same species.

• Most fish prefer the size and color pattern of partners of the same species and withdraw from other fish.

• Individual species, and often even subspecies and populations, have developed their own mating behavior. Both sexes react optimally only when

mating with their own species. The lack of affinity between sexual partners of different species places so severe a strain on them that they soon abandon the fruitless endeavor and seek a suitable partner of their own species. In the aquarium these barriers to crossbreeding may be ignored if no breeding partner of the same species is available. This is especially true of some species of fish that bear live young (see page 103) and of killifish (in this group the females of many species look almost alike: see page 95).

Avoid Undesirable Crossbreeding

• Do not keep species that crossbreed together in the community tank.

• Never keep aquarium-bred and wild forms of species together. The young of such varied parentage usually have poor coloring and show neither the marked characteristics of the bred or the wild form.

• When purchasing killifish be sure that the females belong to the same species as the males, even if you obtain them from the same breeder or if they originate from the same habitat.

• If you find recently introduced, unknown fish at a pet shop or importer, ask where they came from. Breed them, where possible, only with fish from the same habitat.

• If you are engaged in maintaining an endangered population, you should not introduce members from other populations. This prevents diluting the genetic potential of different populations.

Labyrinth fish that build foam nests
Stages in the reproductive behavior of the dwarf gourami (*Colisa lalia*).
Above left: The male establishes his territory and builds a foam nest.
Above right: Shortly before spawning, the female approaches for clasping.
Below left: During mating the male and female turn sideways and emit their eggs and sperm.
Below right: As the eggs start sinking (left in the photo), the male collects them in his mouth and spits them into the foam nest.

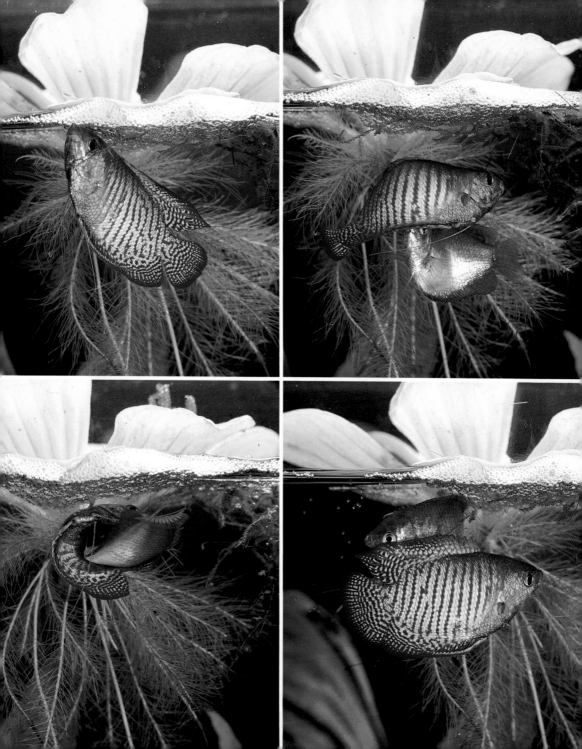

About Breeding Fish

The Consequences of Domestication

If a species of fish is bred for generations in an aquarium, it may develop new color patterns, fin shapes, or forms of behavior. However, it may also lose behavior patterns and physical properties that are essential for survival in the wild if such qualities are not necessary for survival in an aquarium.

Example: Most tropical fish spawn at the beginning of the rainy season. At that time rivers flood their banks, and huge numbers of bacteria, algae, and other organisms develop in the inundated areas. These serve as the first source of food for the hatchlings. Signals that alert the fish to the appropriate time for spawning are tropical storms, an increase in the water level, the decrease of water hardness (when the river water is diluted by an immense amount of rainwater), an altered food supply, and so on. Under natural conditions fish spawn only when all these factors come together. Were they to reproduce during other periods, their young would develop under unfavorable water conditions and with an insufficient food supply, thus reducing future generations.

The aquarium hobbyist prefers fish with modest environmental requirements. These fish can spawn without receiving the necessary signals from the environment. Breeders are happy to possess such "good pairs" that enable them to breed as many offspring as possible and distribute them to other breeders. This can result in the creation of fish varieties that are unable to survive in the wild.

Fish breeding in the aquarium, thus, results in domestication; the aquarium fish develop into "house pets." As more generations flourish in the aquarium, more "house pet" qualities are produced. Aquarium guppies, for instance, are much larger than the wild relatives. Male guppies with veil fins can barely mate with females. Conspicuous albino (white) and golden yellow breeds would soon be devoured in the wild.

Very striking mating behavior
These mouthbreeding fighting fish (*Betta macrophthalma*) appear to be in a loving embrace. The mating behavior of other species is less striking. Since eggs and sperm are emitted during the embrace, the closeness of the fish ensures that almost all of the eggs will be fertilized.

Aquarium Tanks and Equipment

If you want to breed fish, one aquarium will not be sufficient. You will need at least one additional tank in which to isolate the young so that they will not be eaten by the other inhabitants of the aquarium. Depending on the species of fish involved, you may need more than two aquariums—sometimes many more.

Tanks Adapted for Breeding

For fish breeding—just as for general maintenance—the glass aquarium bonded with silicon rubber is best. It is easy to keep clean and (when necessary) to disinfect. The tank size depends on the needs of the fish species that you want to breed. (For precise instructions, see pages 70 to 132.) Make sure that the cover fits well, as fish very often jump quite high during mating.

Community Aquariums

These are probably the best for most beginning hobbyists. Labyrinth fish, catfish, cichlids and others can also spawn there, but the offspring for the most part will be quickly devoured by the other tank occupants. Community aquariums are therefore unsuited for fish breeding.

Species Aquarium

Tanks designed for the needs of a specific species of fish create the most natural living conditions possible and permit the inhabitants to exhibit their complete repertory of behavior. As a result, such tanks often enable the aquarist to make extremely interesting observations. Species aquariums are particularly well suited for fish with interesting brood care behavior (such as cichlids and labyrinth fish), fish that care little for their brood (such as salmon), and fish with unusual spawning behavior (such as butterfly fish). After spawning, the eggs of the brood-caring species should be given to the parents for rearing. The eggs of the fish that do not care for their spawn are removed from the species tank and transferred to a rearing tank.

Spawning Tanks

Spawning tanks are containers into which certain fish from community or species tanks are assigned for the purpose of reproduction. After spawning the fish are returned to the maintenance tank. This method is best for species that simply strew their eggs into the aquarium or among plants. Such fish are encouraged to spawn as pairs or in small groups in this auxiliary tank. Some of the most popular of the species that do not tend their young are the characins, barbs, and other small fish of the carp type. In the spawning tank the special needs of the fish (water quality, for example) can be more easily controlled.

Rearing Tanks

Rearing tanks help in the rearing of the brood. A spawning tank in which eggs develop after the parents have been lured out serves as an aquarium for rearing the young during the first few days of life. Rearing tanks contain water whose quality corresponds to that of the breeding water. Small rearing tanks are easier to keep clean and the live food in such tanks is more easily accessible to the young. As the fry grow older, they need larger tanks in which they will have clean water and room to grow up.

Breeding Setups

If you breed fish regularly and need many spawning and rearing tanks of the same size, you may want to link the tanks together into stands and cases. There are many types of stable metal cases that you can put together yourself. The tanks should not be placed directly on metal supports or on the metal stand surfaces. A styrofoam base is just as important here as it is in the construction of individual aquariums. A breeding setup is more convenient to service than small individual tanks which are distributed around the house. In addition, you can use technical equipment such as heating and lighting for several tanks at the same time.

Aquarium Tanks and Equipment

Construction of the Aquarium

Aquariums need a firm foundation that will not buckle under the weight of the filled tank. A styrofoam base will be compressed by the weight of the aquarium, and its "give" will take care of any remaining unevenness and secure the bottom of the tank.

Beware of the weight. Don't forget that a gallon of water weighs eight pounds and that the weight of an aquarium corresponds to its cubic volume in gallons.

You can determine the volume of an aquarium by using the following formula:

$$\frac{length \times width \times height\ (in\ inches)}{231} = \text{Volume in gallons.}$$

Multiply this figure by 8 and add the weight of the empty tank to get the total weight of the tank and its water.

A breeding setup can be even heavier than a well-filled bookcase.

Therefore, before constructing a large breeding setup, find out about the load-bearing capacity of the floors in your house.

My suggestion: If possible, place your aquarium in the basement. It should have a water supply and, most important, a floor drain. In addition, you should be able to heat and ventilate the room. A latex-based wall paint retards damage to wall plaster due to dampness.

Technical Equipment

Water temperature, quality, and cleanliness play an important role in the breeding and rearing of fish. You will be ble to meet the requirements for specific fish species by using heaters, lamps, and filters. Electrical heating and safety systems made especially for aquarium setups are available from various manufacturers. Ask in the tropical fish store about the best equipment for your needs. Regardless of any safety systems used, always unplug all electrical equipment before you reach into the water.

My suggestion: Purchase only Underwriters Laboratory (UL) approved equipment for the construction of the breeding setup. Electrical equipment in the aquarium must carry the statement that it can be safely used under water.

Sumatra barbs during mating. All barbs require plants with fine branches in the breeding tank.

Heating

During breeding many fish require an increase in temperature of about 2 to 5°F (1 to 3°C).

• If you're breeding fish in the species tank, you need only raise the setting of your heater thermostat to the new temperature.

• Small and medium spawning and rearing tanks are heated by electric immersion heaters with built-in thermostats. They are available in various wattages based on the size of the tank.

• If you wish to control an entire array of large breeding tanks of equal size you can also obtain heaters without built-in thermostats and connect them all jointly to a single thermostat.

• If the temperature required for breeding is not too high, you can get along without a heating device by adjusting the room temperature to the desired aquarium temperature. The aquarium water will approximate this temperature, and there will be less water condensation in the room and on the aquarium glass. In general, professional breeders always heat the aquarium rooms and seldom the tanks themselves.

• Every tank should be equipped with a thermostat for controlling of the temperature.

• You will find precise instructions on the optimal temperature for individual species of fish in the chapter "Breeding Instructions for Aquarium Fish" (see pages 70 to 132).

Lighting

Fish in the aquarium reproduce only when they have an overall sense of well-being. Among other things this means that they need somewhere between 12 and 14 hours of daylight. This corresponds to the length of the day in the tropics and subtropical regions, the habitat from which the fish originate. The production of sexual hormones that regulate the reproduction of the fish depends upon maintaining these daylight hours.

Breeding in species or community tanks. If you breed in these tanks make no changes in the existing lighting setup as this would upset the fish.

Small spawning tanks. If you breed only rarely and have one or two breeding tanks from which the breeding pairs are removed immediately after spawning and returned to the regular tanks, you can do without a regular light for the tank and can use a desk lamp with a medium-strength light bulb. Be sure that the light—which the fish have become accustomed to—shines down from above and that there is a protective covering between the bulb and the water to prevent the water from being heated by the lamp.

Larger breeding aquariums. The best light source for these is from fluorescent lights. It is best to use the same type of tube that you use in the maintenance tank of this fish species.

Fish that love the morning sun. Many fish, particularly those from intensely sunny waters —

such as, for example, Celebes rainbow fish (*Telmatherina ladigesi*), most *Corydorus* catfish species and many cichlids — spawn readily when the morning sun shines on the tank. Therefore, place the breeding tank so that the morning sun shines on it, whether the aquarium is lit artificially or not lit at all.

Bichirs during mating. The male (above) forms his anal fin into a pocket to catch the eggs.

Fish that are sensitive to light. Professional breeders keep these fish in a form of twilight and keep the tank dark by covering it with paper or cardboard. This technique is also recommended for the amateur breeder. A word of caution: When the young have departed from their parents you may restore the light very slowly over a period of several days.

Characins and barbs (such as the red neon and Harlequin fish) are particularly sensitive to light, (see pages 71 and 81).

Aquarium Tanks and Equipment

Filter and Ventilation

A filter as well as a steady supply of oxygen are as important in breeding and rearing aquariums as in community tanks. In addition, the filter and aerator produce a permanent flow of moving water that induces many fish species to mate.

How Does a Filter Work?

The filter mechanically removes suspended matter such as food particles and fish droppings. Nitrogen-fixing bacteria settle on the filter bed (see page 16). These bacteria transform poisonous nitrites—produced from ammonia (in alkaline water) and ammonium ions (in acidic water), which accumulate from the decomposition of food and fish secretions—into relatively harmless nitrates. Such "bacterial denitrification" requires oxygen. You should therefore make sure that the water always contains sufficient oxygen (see page 16).

The Right Filter

The choice of inside or outside filters has little bearing on your chances for success in breeding. It is also unimportant whether your filters are powered by gyroscope pumps, motors, or air pumps. It is vital, however, that you obtain equipment whose water flow can be regulated. Filters in breeding and rearing aquariums should often run very slowly so that eggs and sperm are not sucked in. Therefore, buy filters whose power can be varied. The following are suggestions for different types of tanks.

Large species aquariums, in which you may wish to keep and breed cichlids, catfish, or other large fish for their entire lives, should be fitted with a gyroscope-propelled outside filter or an inside filter that is capable of high output.

Smaller species tanks that are used for maintenance as well as breeding (as in the case of labyrinth fish) need slow filters that produce few currents.

Spawning tanks, in which the fish spend only a few hours or days, are just 8 to 24 inches (20–60 cm) long and do not require a powerful filter. Usually the fish are not fed in these tanks. Thus we recommend small, gentle filters powered by vibrating membrane pumps or inside filters with an adjustable motor. The membrane pumps that operate the small filters are not as noisy as they were 20 years ago. Membrane pumps of various sizes can take care of one or several small filters that also have aeration outflows. If you own just a few breeding tanks, you can make do with a large vibrating membrane pump or a few smaller ones. If, however, these pumps are used constantly, the membranes should be changed every few months. Many breeders have no filters at all in spawning tanks.

Rearing aquariums require very efficient filters that can be cleaned quickly and easily. Avoid filters with powerful suction, since they can draw the spawn into the filter material. Yet the filters must be efficient enough to remove the large amount of organic material (which can decompose to ammonia or nitrates) generated by intense feeding and fish droppings. Ammonia- and nitrate-laden water impede the growth of the brood. Light-duty pumps and filters are well suited for these aquariums, as the bubble flow is so fine that the fry do not wander into it. These pumps can easily be dismantled, washed, and put back into the tank. You can make use of any type of inside filter if you slow down the output.

If you are concerned that your fry will be caught in the suction of the filter, you can cover the intake or the entire filter with a gauze cloth. You must clean this netting thoroughly in fresh water at least once a day.

My suggestion: When the fry begin to swim freely, keep them for the first few days in a tank with a slow filter. As soon as they have become somewhat larger and stronger, put them in a bigger rearing tank with a motor driven inside filter. If you rear the fry in containers in which filtering is impossible (for example, in photographic developing tanks; see page 93) you should exchange practically all the water for fresh water of the same quality on a daily basis.

Aquarium Tanks and Equipment

Ancistrus males (sucker-mouth armored catfish family) are devoted fathers. They not only care for the eggs but also for the young until they are about 0.4 inch (1 cm) long.

Filter Materials

Filter materials commonly found in aquariums can also be used in breeding tanks. Two of these serve very specific functions.

Peat acidifies the water and softens it. Peat filtering is very effective for breeding fish from tropical rain forests, where the water produces a high amount of humic acid from foliage, deadwood, and other plant material. For these fish filter the water in the spawning tank over peat for three days and then return the fish to the tank.

Instead of peat, extracts can be used by simply adding the appropriate amount for the volume of water in the tank. They are easier to use but often are not as effective as filtering the water over peat.

Activated charcoal is required for breeding fish that produce many eggs and large amounts of sperm and seminal fluid, for example, penguin fish (*Thayeria boehlkei*) and glass tetra (*Moenkhausia oligolepis*). When the eggs are fertilized, you must filter the water for several hours over activated charcoal to remove the surplus sperm. When the sperm die, they decompose and spoil the water. This can induce abundant growth of bacteria and fungi, which could destroy the entire egg nest. Do not filter the water when the fish are spawning; this would draw a part of the sperm into the filter. Fish eggs are viable for only a few minutes, so wait a while after spawning and then insert the filter. Activated charcoal often is not enough when dealing with an especially large egg nest; in such cases disinfectants must be added.

My suggestion: You can frequently avoid the use of disinfectants by preparing a tank equal in size to the spawning tank, filling it with similar water, and keeping it at the same temperature. It should also be filtered. After spawning, if the eggs are on the bottom of the tank (and not clinging to the walls), you can remove almost all the water from the spawning tank and then pour in the clean, warmed water from the second tank. This will remove the bulk of the sperm, and the activated charcoal will filter out the remnants.

Aeration of the Breeding Tank

Lack of oxygen can lead to the death of fertilized eggs. Since slow filters in breeding and rearing aquariums often pump too little oxygen, you should use airstones in these tanks. They consist of material with very fine pores connected by a plastic tube to a membrane pump. The pump forces air through the tube into the airstone, and the air bubbles out through the tiny pores in the stone. The finer the pores, the smaller the bubbles. Small individual bubbles have a greater surface area, which permits more oxygen to be absorbed by the water. Especially fine airstones can be made from linden wood.

Why a Water Current is Important for Breeding

Filters and aeration create a strong water current, which is essential to breeding for several reasons. For many species of fish—in particular those from rivers and streams and those that undertake spawning journeys (mostly upstream), such as loaches and large salmon—a strong water current is the trigger for spawning. If you keep such fish in the species or community tank, you must use a gyroscope pump to produce a current. This is particularly important in the two months before the rainy season would have begun in the wild.

In addition, the water motion mixes the aquarium water so that water layers with different temperatures cannot form.

Parasites and fungi do not thrive in flowing water; thus water motion also helps to avoid diseases.

Additional Equipment

This section contains information about non-technical additions to breeding tanks such as the tank bed, decorative branches, rocks, plants, and spawning aids.

The Tank Bed

Species aquariums for fish that care for their brood are constructed according to the needs of their occupants. They are planted and contain a normal ground surface.

Spawning tanks for those species whose brood is highly sensitive to bacteria and infusorians should not have a tank bed. With less sensitive species it does no harm.

For sensitive species (for instance, cardinal tetra, jewel tetra, emperor tetra) paint the tank floor with a dark paint or cover it with dark paper, dark fabric, or a dark colored styrofoam plate to eliminate reflection, which can disturb these fish during spawning. Fish that eat their eggs after spawning need a spawning grate (see page 21). For less sensitive species make a tank bed from sand sterilized by boiling or baking in an oven. Seasonal egg-laying killifish that spawn on the ground (see page 95) should be provided with a relatively thick layer of well-moistened peat in which to lay their eggs. The thickness of the layer depends on the spawning behavior of the particular species (see page 97).

Rearing tanks. Avoid a tank bed or use only a thin layer of sand so that these cc cleaned more easily.

Spawning Beds and Oth

Species aquariums. Brood-to cichlids, many catfish, or labyrinth their own spawning places in the species tank, where they watch over the eggs and young. The demands that they make on the spawning bed vary from species to species. Usually, these fish are content with substitute materials.

• Vertical or diagonal stone disks or flat stones serve as spawning places for open breeders among the cichlids (see page 111). You can also substitute tiles.

• The more secretive cichlids (see page 111) and brood-tending catfish (see page 89) require caves in stones or roots for their eggs and young. However, these fish will also use plastic tubing, hollowed-out coconut shells, or flowerpots for their caves.

• Some fish make use of plant stems (see page 95) as spawning places. However, you can also substitute rods made of green glass.

• Splash tetras, for example, need plant leaves for attaching their egg nest (see page 78). However, they will also use green glass or green pieces of styrofoam.

Spawning tanks for the most part do not contain spawning beds. When setting these up, however, always provide spawning plants (see page 22) or a spawning grate (see page 21). Only when breeding aggressive species of fish (for example, egg-laying killifish) will you require a few roots or stone tiles necessary as hiding places for the females.

Breeding tanks require no spawning beds.

My suggestion: Prior to being used in the aquarium, roof tiles, flowerpots, and all other tile material must be soaked in water and peat for an entire day (2 gallons of water, 2 handfuls of peat). The humic acid in the peat neutralizes the toxic aluminum compounds that may be present in new tiles. Use as many natural components as possible in the species tanks so that the fish will be bred in a natural environment.

s in the Breeding Aquarium

ts are needed not only in the species aquari-
ns, which are furnished with tank beds, stones,
branches, roots, and so on; they also belong in
spawning aquariums, in which the fish spend only
a few days. In tanks without tank beds (see page
17) the plants may be weighted down with glass
rods or glass beads so that they do not float up to
the surface. Plants are not necessary in rearing
tanks for the newly spawned young; in rearing
tanks for older fry they may be placed in small
flowerpots. These are not needed when there is a
tank bed.

*Plants perform various functions in the
breeding aquarium.*

• Many plants serve as spawning places for fish,
which fasten their eggs to the plants (piece by
piece or in small batches) after they have cleaned
the leaves or stalks.

• Plants can also serve as accidental spawning
places for schools of fish that dart through the thick
plant growth during mating and strew their eggs
about at random. Because of their adhesive
properties, the eggs cling to the plant leaves.

• Plants—especially those with dense, fine
foliage—possess a large surface area and can emit
a large amount of oxygen into the water and take
up a large amount of carbon dioxide.

• Many types of plants use large amounts of
ammonia or nitrates, which are produced as waste
products by fish and are often toxic to them.

• All plants destroy bacteria in the water.

• Plants serve as protection for female fish, which
are often ardently chased during mating.

Choose the right plants.

• Spawning plants should correspond to the
spawning habits of the fish.

• They should be appropriate for the quality and
temperature of the water.

The most important spawning plants are found on
pages 22 to 24.

Clean the Spawning Plants

Water plants can be added to the aquarium along
with slugs, small nematodes, and planaria.

In species aquariums for brood-tending fish, such

creatures are no threat to the eggs and young in the
daytime because the parents will eat them or
remove them from the eggs. At night, however,
they can be a threat to the eggs of brood-tending
species.

In spawning and rearing tanks fish that do not tend
their brood can attack the spawn and destroy the
entire egg mass. The spawn of many types of fish
is very sensitive to bacteria, fungi, and infusorians.
These organisms not only attack the eggs directly,
but also harm them by depriving them of oxygen.

Therefore, wash the plants carefully under running
water; for sensitive fish species disinfect them in
an alum bath. If you have enough room, you can
construct an additional tank free of fish and slugs
for the cultivation of spawning plants. All damaged
leaves and stem parts should be carefully removed
so they will not decompose.

Plant Substitutes

If you have extremely sensitive fish that must be
bred under almost sterile conditions you can use a
spawning web made of green synthetic fibers. It
looks somewhat like green algae. This may be too
hard for many fish, and they can become disori-
ented when spawning in it. Egg-laying killifish that
attach their eggs by suction particularly dislike
these spawning webs.

Alternatively, you can use spawning fans. These
are fiber clusters tied around a plastic tube. The

Spawning of cave-breeding cichlids. The spawning
caves of cichlids do not always have an opening large
enough for the larger male to fit through. The female
(top) spawns in the cave, the male spawns near the
opening. The sperm flow to the eggs with the water.
In the case of the purple cichlid (*Pelvichromis
pulcher*) the parents jointly share the rearing tasks.
The female cares for the eggs, while the male guards
the territory.

Aquarium Tanks and Equipment

tube is placed diagonally over the tank, and the fiber clusters dangle into the tank like small, limp brooms. The fish are attracted to these fans and deposit their eggs on them. Long peat clusters fastened to the tank cover work in a similar fashion.

Spawning Grates and Spawning Boxes
Spawning grates and spawning boxes are devices designed to prevent the parents from eating their own eggs and fry.
Spawning grates are laid on the tank floor so that the eggs fall into the hollow space and are protected from the pursuing parents. Here are some variations:
• The simplest spawning grate is a layer of glass marbles on a thin layer of sand. Eggs lying between the marbles are not easily sucked up.
• You can place loose glass rods on the tank floor to form a lattice. Short glass rods (corresponding to the width of the tank) should be placed on the narrow side of the tank floor. Long glass rods (corresponding to the length of the tank) are laid across them at intervals of about 0.1 inch (2–3 mm). The eggs will fall through the openings onto the tank floor, where they will be protected from predators. You can obtain the glass rods from a laboratory supply store. They can be pasted together with a waterproof glue.
All spawning grates and the sand layer that goes under the glass marbles must be heated for a few hours in a baking oven.
Spawning boxes have a built-in grate. Female live bearers, such as killifish, bear their young in there. The newborn fall through the grate into the lower section of the box and are thus protected from attack by the mother. Unfortunately, most of the spawning boxes are too small, and the females—at least those of the larger species (platy and larger)—often get so excited in the tiny containers that they drop their young too early. It is recommended that breeders of live-bearing killifish construct larger spawning boxes themselves.

My suggestion: With fish that abandon their young, the parents should be taken out after spawning, and the eggs can remain in the spawning tank until they hatch. With fish that spawn over a period of days or weeks, the eggs should be carefully sucked up with a hose and transferred into the rearing tank.

Angelfish laying eggs. Golden angelfish (*Pterophyllum scalare*) belong to the family of perch; they spawn on oblique or flat surfaces. Here they are using the wide leaves of an Amazon swordplant (*Echinodorus*).

The Most Important Spawning Plants

Cabomba caroliniana
Fanwort, fish grass
Stem plants whose leaf spread is finely plumed. Hardiest *Cabomba* species with the least light requirements.
Water: 72–82°F (22–28°C); 2–12 dH; pH 6.5–7.2
Maintenance: Planted, anchored with glass rods or free-floating.
Spawning plant for many barbs and characins.

Ceratophyllum demersum
Hornwort
Rootless stem plants with bifurcated, parted leaves. Hardy.
Water: 59–86°F (15–30°C); 5–15 dH; pH 6–7.5
Maintenance: Free floating (forms thick cushion under the water surface), or anchored to the floor with glass rods.
Spawning plant for all fish. Also provides hiding place for females and fry.

Ceratopteris thalictroides
Water sprite
Deeply feathered streamlined leaf spread. Big finely ramified root system.
Water: 68–86°F (20–30°C); 2–12 dH; pH 6.5–7.5
Maintenance: Planted, anchored with glass rods, or free floating.
Spawning plant for all larger and foam nest-building fish.

Cryptocoryne affinis
Hardiest *Cryptocoryne* species. Medium to large.
Water: 72–82°F (22–28°C); 3–15 dH; pH 6–7.5
Maintenance: Potted or planted.
Spawning plant for fish that spawn on the top or bottom side of broad leaves.

Echinodorus bleheri
Amazon swordplant.
Model for many *Echinodorus* species. Requires more light than *Cryptocoryne* species. A big plant.
Water: 72–82°F (22–28°C); 2–15 dH; pH 6.5–7.5.
Maintenance: Potted or planted.
Spawning plant for fish that spawn on the top or bottom side of broad leaves. Particularly useful for larger fish, such as angelfish.

Egeria densa
Argentinian waterweed
Stem plants with tiny leaves.
Water: 59–77°F (15–25°C); 8–15 dH; pH 6.5–7.5.
Maintenance: Free-floating.
Spawning plant for free-spawning fish in colder water.

The Most Important Spawning Plants

Eichhornia crassipes
Water hyacinth
Grows to 14 inches (35 cm) in height above the water level. Root bushes are spawning beds and a refuge for fry.
Water: 72–82°F (22–28°C); 2–15 dH; pH 6–7.8.
Maintenance: Floating. Requires much light.
Spawning plant ideal for foam nests of labyrinth fish. Also provides shade.

Hygrophila difformis
Indian water star
High stem plant. Roots at the stem joints.
Water: 72-82°F (22-28°C); 2-15 dH; pH 6.5-7.5.
Maintenance: Planted or free-floating. Needs plenty of light.
Spawning plant for larger free-spawning fish.

Limnophila sessiliflora.
High stem plant with leaves having a vertical swirl.
Water: 72-82°F (22-28°C); 3–15 dH; pH 6-7.5.
Maintenance: Planted or free-floating. Requires light to survive.
Spawning plant for all free-spawning characins and barbs.

Ludwigia palustris and repens (natans)
Needle-leaf and green Ludwigia
Unpretentious. Suitable for cold water tanks.
Water: 63–82°F (17–28°C); 3–15 dH; pH 5.8–7.5.
Maintenance: Planted or free-floating.
Spawning plant for fish that like to spawn on smaller leaf surfaces (for example, chessboard cichlids).

Myriophyllum aquaticum
Soft, fine-plumed leaves.
Water: 64–86°F (18–30°C), 2–15 dH; pH 6–7.5.
Maintenance: Planted or anchored with glass rods.
Spawning plant for small free spawners.

Najas guadelupensis
Najas microdon
Leaves are small and thin.
Water: 72–82°F (22–28°C); 2–12 dH; pH 6–7.5.
Maintenance: As free floating cushioning under the water surface.
Spawning plant for small, gentle fish and as a refuge for fry of live-bearing killifish.

The Most Important Spawning Plants

Pistia stratiotes
Water lettuce
Grows to 12 inches (30 cm) on the average. Root masses (smaller than those of *the water hyacinth*) serve as spawning beds and refuge for fry.
Water: 72–79°F (22–26°C); 5–15 dH; pH 6.5–7.5.
Maintenance: Floating plant. Requires aerated water.
Spawning plant for foam nest builders and killifish.

Potamogeton gayii
Stem plants with small leaves.
Water: 68–86°F (20–30°C); 2–12 dH; pH 6–7.2.
Maintenance: Planted or anchored with glass rods.
Spawning plant for free spawners.

Riccia fluitans
Crystalwort
Flat, bifurcate branchings that bind together to form thick cushions.
Water: 59–86°F (15–30°C); 5–15 dH; pH 6–8.
Maintenance: Floating plant.
Spawning plant for labyrinth fish (as building material and anchorage for foam nests). Ideal refuge for fry.

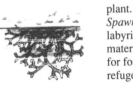

Sagittaria subulata
Plants with ribbonlike leaves. Many varieties with different leaf widths.
Water: 68–82°F (20–28°C;) 2–15 dH; pH 6–7.8.
Maintenance: Planted, anchored with glass rods, or floating.
Spawning plant for needle catfish.

Vallisneria spiralis
Ribbonlike leaves forming branches.
Water: 59–86°F (15–30°C); 5–12 dH; pH 6.5–7.5.
Maintenance: Planted, anchored with glass rods, or floating.
Spawning plant for many fish with adhesive spawn (for example, salmon).

Vesicularia dubyana
Java moss
Thin–stemmed foliage moss. Develops luxuriantly and forms thick padding.
Water: 68–86°F (20–30°C); 2–15 dH; pH 5.8–7.5.
Maintenance: Padding on the floor anchored with glass rods. Does not require much light.
Spawning plant for small free-spawning fish such as barbs, characins, and rainbow fish.

The Water Environment

In fish breeding the quality of the water is an essential criterion for success or failure. Water not only triggers the urge to reproduce but is also the "foundation" of the whole reproductive process. Water, with few exceptions, is the environment in which fertilization takes place and the embryo develops from egg to larva to fry. For optimal breeding you must provide the fish with water conditions to which they are accustomed and that resemble as closely as possible those of their natural habitat.

Exact water analyses are indispensable for breeding. They have become much easier in recent years with the development of different measuring techniques. Testing strips or testing tabs can be used quickly and without difficulty.

Below is a list of the major properties of water that can be adjusted precisely to the needs of the fish. They will be discussed in detail in this chapter.

• Gases dissolved in water such as oxygen (O_2) and carbon dioxide (CO_2).

• The water hardness or the mineral content (salt content) of the water. This is directly related to the osmotic pressure.

• The pH, which measures the acidity of the water.

• The content of organic substances (see page 34), and in particular the nitrogenous products of metabolism (protein, ammonia, ammonium, nitrite, nitrate). These are produced by the decomposition of food and animal remains and are excreted by fish in urine and feces. Organic substances are also produced by the decomposition of plants and by peat formation. They acidify the water and give swamp and tropical water its typical brown color. Tropical fish shops sell extracts enriched in these materials, which you can add to the aquarium water.

Gases Dissolved in Water

Oxygen (O_2) and carbon dioxide (CO_2) are essential for all aquarium inhabitants.

Oxygen

All animals and plants take up oxygen and give off carbon dioxide. Oxygen is absorbed by the water from air and (during daylight), through the photosynthesis of plants. Plants themselves require oxygen for respiration, but during the day they produce about five times as much oxygen as they need. Since the plants give off oxygen only in daylight (in the aquarium also under bright illumination), there are large variations in oxygen content between day and night. The oxygen is at its lowest level in the morning, it increases during the day, and drops off sharply at night.

What you should know about oxygen

• The more vigorous the movement of the water, the more oxygen it can absorb from the air. In nature this movement is caused by winds and currents; in the aquarium by filtering and aeration.

• Oxygen dissolves much better in cold water than in warm water. Fish from cool, rapidly flowing water therefore need more oxygen than those from stagnant ponds that are heated by the sun.

• Oxygen is also needed by bacteria that decompose the nitrogenous waste products of the fish (ammonia) into harmless substances (nitrates).

• The oxygen content can be determined with testing kits or an electronic measuring apparatus (both can be obtained in a tropical fish supply store). It should not fall below 4 mg per liter (quart) of water in the average maintenance tank.

• A persistently low oxygen level in water may be due to too many fish and too few plants in the aquarium, overfeeding, neglecting to change the water in the aquarium, or the presence of too much organic matter in the water or in the filter, so that nitrogen decomposition cannot take place.

What to do about lack of oxygen. When the lack of oxygen in the water is acute, the fish gasp for air at the water surface. This behavior can also be caused by ammonia or nitrite poisoning (see Ammonia and Nitrite, page 35).

To remedy a lack of oxygen; do the following:

• Perform a partial water change (four-fifths of the tank contents). This must be done slowly.

• Put hydrogen peroxide in the water (25 ml of a 3 percent hydrogen peroxide solution to 29 gallons (100 liters) of aquarium water). Add the hydrogen peroxide only once; if done repeatedly, it will poison the fish.

Tetras are fastidious breeders. Since they do not take care of their eggs, the water must be especially clean. In this photo we see glowlight tetra spawning.

• Oxygen supplement tablets (available in tropical fish stores) may be used according to the dosage instructions on the package. If the fish are already gasping for breath, it makes no sense to turn on the filter or aerators more strongly. This will only stir up the debris in the tank and further reduce the oxygen content.

Important advice for breeding. Eggs, sperm, and embryos need more oxygen than adult fish.

• The oxygen content in the breeding tank should not fall below 4 mg per liter (quart) of water.

• Put plants that are good oxygen producers (such as water-weed) in every breeding aquarium.

• In breeding aquariums in which no plants can be placed the oxygen content can be maintained by powerful filtering, water movement, or partial daily water changes.

Carbon Dioxide

Carbon dioxide (CO_2) also dissolves in water. It is absorbed from the air and is exhaled by fish,

plants, and bacteria. Carbon dioxide is released by the decomposition of bacteria and other organisms and is a by-product of the metabolism of nitrogen compounds, which are formed from fish urine and feces and the decomposition of food. Moreover, CO_2 is vital for plant nutrition. Without it the plants cannot assimilate and form oxygen, which the fish and filter bacteria need for life.

Additional facts about carbon dioxide. A too high CO_2 content can occur in the morning in tanks with many fish and plants. Sloppy eaters, too much debris on the floor of the tank, and a very dirty filter likewise raise the CO_2 content.

The CO_2 can be removed from the water by powerful aeration, which vigorously agitates the water surface.

Important for breeding.

• When breeding brood-tending fish in planted aquariums (whether in community or species tanks) do not overstock them with fish. If you provide a large number of plants, the water will remain fairly clean. Eggs, sperm, and embryos will develop without difficulty.

• Do not put plants (or use only a few) in species aquariums for herbivorous fish or in breeding tanks for fish that require bacteria-free water. Such tanks must be thoroughly aerated. Good aeration is also needed in breeding aquariums with weak light, in which the plants cannot produce oxygen (this is important, for instance, in the breeding of neon tetras).

• Considerable amounts of CO_2 are formed in rearing aquariums for fry, in which (due to the dense habitation and heavy feeding) large amounts of fish droppings and food particles fall constantly. In tanks with newly hatched young, change the water daily if possible. Tanks for older fry should be well planted and filtered vigorously. A partial water change daily is essential.

Water Hardness

In nature water contains large amounts of mineral salts that are absorbed from underground sources. Salts are chemical compounds formed from metals (calcium, sodium, potassium, magnesium, iron, and so on) and acids (carbonic acid, sulfuric acid, nitric acid, and so on). Water hardness is determined by its content of alkaline-earth metal salts, primarily by calcium and magnesium salts. Water is considered hard if it contains a large amount of these salts and soft if the salt concentration is small.

Water hardness is expressed in degrees of hardness (dH). Each degree corresponds to 30 mg of calcium or magnesium carbonate per liter (quart) of water.

The following scale expresses water hardness in dH units:

0–4 dH = very soft water
5–8 dH = soft water
9–12 dH = medium hard water
13–20 dH = hard water
20 dH and up = very hard water

Other scales may be employed by manufacturers of kits for testing water hardness. Find out the degree of hardness of your tap water from your water supply company. In many places, water from different sources is mixed according to the water needs of the community, so that on different days the water can have completely different degrees of hardness. Thus, you should measure the hardness of the water yourself.

Aquarium fish, plants, and filter bacteria thrive best in water with a general hardness of about 8 to 16 dH. Normal tap water also has this value. Therefore, if you limit yourself to the maintenance of fish, you can get by with tap water.

Important for breeding. For breeding purposes the water properties should correspond to those found in the natural habitat of the fish species.

• Almost all fish from tropical forests will breed in water with a hardness of between 3 and 6 dH.

• Softer water is needed only for extremely specialized types, such as discus fish or cardinal tetras.

• Cichlids from East Africa and Central America as well as many other less fastidious fish will breed in medium hard to hard water.

• The orange chromide of the genus *Etroplus* as well as the giant sailfin molly *Poecilia velifera*

need brackish water or the addition of a sea salt supplement.

Carbonate and Noncarbonate Hardness
The general hardness of the water consists of carbonate hardness (CH) and the noncarbonate hardness (NCH). Carbonate hardness is due to the presence of carbonates and bicarbonates (calcium and magnesium salts of the carbonic acids). The carbonate hardness can be eliminated by boiling the water, which precipitates the salts until they are no longer measurable. Thus, carbonate hardness was previously known as "temporary hardness." The "permanent hardness" of the water after boiling is called noncarbonate hardness and is due primarily to the presence of calcium and magnesium sulfate. This was previously referred to as "sulfate hardness."

Carbonate hardness has a more drastic effect on the well-being of fish and plants than noncarbonate hardness. It affects the pH value of the water (see page 32), the CO_2 content, and the plants. Some plant species (such as waterweed and *Vallisneria*) can remove carbon dioxide from the carbonates and bicarbonates if too little CO_2 is dissolved in the water. But this raises the pH so much that the fish can perish. Therefore, carbonate hardness in planted aquariums should be measured about once a week.

Measuring carbonate hardness. In a pet shop or laboratory supply store you can obtain special drop indicators for measuring carbonate hardness. Logically the carbonate hardness cannot be higher than the general hardness. However, with drop indicators the carbonate hardness frequently shows a higher value than the general hardness. This is not a measuring error and it doesn't mean that the testing kit is useless. It indicates that, in addition to calcium and magnesium salts, other salts (such as sodium and potassium salts) are dissolved in the water.

Important for breeding.
• Water with a high carbonate hardness is worse than water with a high noncarbonate hardness for breeding of fish used to soft water.

• If the carbonate hardness is under 3 degrees CH

many fish (except the sensitive species) can breed even if salts that cause noncarbonate hardness raise the general hardness above 6 dH.

• Water that is too hard can be made softer by ion exchangers (see page 29) or by peat filtering (see page 30).

• Water that is too soft can be hardened by adding a salt supplement (see page 32).

Osmotic Pressure, General Salt Content, and Conductivity

For fish breeding the general hardness—and thus the sum of all dissolved salts in the water, including table salt and nitrates—is of great importance.

Killifish males in a mouth-to-mouth battle. In this way males of *Nothobranchius* species attempt to drive off rivals.

Osmotic pressure. All animal and plant cells contain a viscous material (the cytoplasm) that contains salts. The salts are responsible for the osmotic pressure of the cell. The cell membrane is porous to water but not to the salts. If the salt concentration—and therefore the osmotic pressure—outside a cell is higher than in its interior, it must give off water to the outside in order to equalize its internal pressure with that of the environment. If the salt concentration in the cell is higher than that outside, the cell takes in water from its surroundings.

In a living organism individual cells usually have the same osmotic pressure. In addition, the living organisms have developed mechanisms to equalize different levels of osmotic pressure.

Adult tropical fish can therefore, be cared for in hard water (water with a high general salt content) even if they are used to softer water. Single cells, on the other hand (such as eggs and sperm), can tolerate only slight deviations of osmotic pressure. In order to be able to survive and develop, they need a water hardness similar to that found in their native habitat.

Example 1: If fish used to soft water spawn in hard water, the osmotic pressure of their eggs and sperm will be lower than that of the water. The cells will then lose water to their surroundings, shrivel, and die.

Example 2: Fish that spawn in water softer than that of their natural habitat yield eggs and sperm whose osmotic pressure is higher than that of the aquarium water. The cells then absorb water and burst.

The general salt content of the water can be quickly determined by measuring its electrical conductivity. The more salt is dissolved in the water, the better it conducts an electric current. Soft water (poor in minerals) thus has a low conductivity; hard water, (rich in minerals) has a high conductivity.

The conductivity is determined by an electric conductivity gauge. It is measured in microiemens per centimeter (μs/cm). The conductivity depends on the water temperature. In order to be able to compare different types of water, the measurements are converted into a uniform temperature; only modern instruments can do this. Conductivity measurements tell nothing about the type of salts dissolved in the water or about their proportions. They only show the general salt content of the water.

The Water Environment

Softening the Water

Medium hard or hard tap water, with a general hardness of 10 to over 30 dH, is not suited for breeding many tropical fish. Salmon, small carp, and many egg-laying killifish and catfish spawn best in soft water (less than 6 dH). Live-bearing killifish and many cichlids multiply freely even in hard tap water.

Important for breeding:
• If you breed fish rarely, you can boil the water to eliminate the carbonate salts, leaving only the noncarbonate salts.
• You can buy distilled water in the drugstore and replace the breeding water with it. If your water consumption is larger, this can be expensive. A cheaper alternative is to buy semi-pure, completely desalted water, which can be obtained on request in many pharmacies.
• Medium hard water can be softened with peat (see page 31).
• The most convenient and economical process for softening large amounts of water is the ion exchange technique.

Ion Exchangers

Ion exchangers can desalt the water completely or only partly.

Ions are electrically charged particles into which salts break down as soon as they dissolve in water. There are two types of ions:

Cations, which originate from the metallic part of the salt, are positively charged.

Anions, which originate from the acidic part of the salt, are negatively charged.

Ion exchangers work on the principle that unlike electrical charges attract each other, and like electrical charges repel each other. Ion exchangers are synthetic resins that swell strongly in water. There are acidic and alkaline (basic) exchange resins.

Acidic exchangers are negatively charged and attract positively charged water ions to them. Basic exchange resins are positively charged and bind negatively charged ions.

Full desalting. Fully desalted water is chemically pure and free of all dissolved salts. It corresponds to distilled water. Full desalting is always necessary when the water hardness is due to carbonate and noncarbonate salts. It is achieved by running tap water first through a cation exchanger and then through an anion exchanger.

Cation exchangers are acid exchangers. Because of their negative electrical charges, they attract all cations. The water is thus freed of all cations; what remain are anions. But since the anions are acid residues, the water is extremely acidic. Therefore, it must be passed through an anion exchanger.

Anion exchangers are basic; because of their positive electrical charge they attract anions. When the water is passed through the anion exchanger, no anions remain, and the water is practically free of all ions. The conductivity is hardly noticeable; for the most part it reads under 0.4 μs/cm.

Partial desalting. If your tap water contains many bicarbonates and carbonates but few other salts, a partial desalting is sufficient to soften the water. You can then use a strongly acidic cation exchanger which will remove all cations from the water.

The number of anions remains unchanged. The water that has been passed through the cation exchanger is acidic (carbonic acid), and therefore has a low pH. The carbonic acid, however, quickly decomposes water and carbon dioxide. The carbon dioxide can be removed quickly if the water from the cation exchanger is whirled around and aerated. Partial desalting works only when almost all of the salt in the water consists of carbonates. If you run water with a high noncarbonate content through a cation exchanger, you will get extremely acidic water in which no fish can survive.

Ion exchange equipment. The size of your ion exchanger and its manufacturer will depend on the quality of your untreated water and upon your water requirements. Precise information on this can be obtained from a tropical fish store.

If you breed only rarely and have small aquariums, you can make do with a small ion exchange cartridge, which is sent to the manufacturer for regeneration. Large-scale users, who breed during the entire year and own many large aquariums, need a large ion exchange setup. Such equipment can supply more than 250 gallons (1000 liters) of water before it is exhausted, and then regenerates itself automatically. Inquire about this at your tropical fish store or read the advertisements in the aquarium magazines.

Birth of a highland carp. The young, born alive, are already fully developed. They have spent the difficult larval period in the protective belly of the mother.

The proper use of the equipment. Ion exchangers are not used on a daily basis but only when water for breeding is being prepared or during periodic partial water changes in all the aquariums.
Here are a few tips for proper usage:
• Never keep the ion exchangers dry after the first usage.
• Do not use the first few quarts of water from the ion exchanger for the aquariums. They contain large amounts of bacteria and fungi that have formed on the wet exchanger resin.
• With small exchanger cartridges you should separate the first 5 to 10 quarts (liters); these can be used for room or balcony plants.

• Owners of larger equipment should collect the first 30 to 50 quarts (liters) for nontank use.
• If you wish to avoid this you can remove the bacteria and fungi from the water by filtering it over activated charcoal or a diatomite filter.
• The fungi and bacteria can also be destroyed by regeneration of the ion exchangers with acids or alkali. However, they will eventually develop again.
Regeneration of the exchangers. The length of time that you can use the ion exchanger depends upon its size, the resin, and the salt content of the water. Ion exchangers usually have electrical indicators to signal when they are exhausted—indicators in the resin that change colors, electrical conductivity indicators or some other mechanism. Exhausted exchangers must be regenerated without fail.
Cation exchangers are regenerated with hydrochloric acid.
Anion exchangers are regenerated with sodium hydroxide (caustic soda) solution.
Acids, bases, and water in a combined washing solution provide an effective mixture. Acids and their rinsing water must be neutralized by sodium hydroxide; bases and their rinsing water must be neutralized by hydrochloric acid. To neutralize means to add enough acid or base so that a pH value of 7 is reached.
Equipment with exchanger cartridges is easier to operate. The exchanger cartridge is sent back to the manufacturing plant (where it is regenerated) as soon as it is exhausted, and the aquarium hobbyist receives another one from the manfacturer.
Fully automatic equipment regenerates itself when the desalted water exceeds a certain electrical conductivity.

Peat
Peat can be used for softening medium-hard water; it has a weak ion exchange capacity. However, peat possesses very favorable qualities for the breeding of tropical fish.
• It acidifies the water.
• It contains hormones.
• It keeps fungi and bacteria from developing in

The Water Environment

the tank.

Softening water with peat.
• Peat obtained from a pet shop is of a different quality than that obtained from a garden supply store. Test the peat before you begin to use it in your breeding water. Never use peat that has been fertilized. For safety's sake, test all peat for manure before using it (see page 34).
• Commercial manure peat, despite its name, is always unfertilized and thus good to use.
• Water will become softened if it is filtered over peat for about 3 days—about 0.5 to 1 quart (liter) peat per 26 gallons (100 liters) of aquarium water. Only then can you put the fish in the water.

Reverse Osmosis

The two methods discussed above for softening water have one disadvantage. Ion exchangers and peat eliminate unwanted salts from the water, but many organic compounds, which do not form ions, pass through the exchanger completely unchanged. Such compounds have recently been found more frequently in the water in recent years. This raises the question of how to protect fish and plants from water contaminated by pesticides and other chemicals.

The apparatus for reverse osmosis is attached to the water faucet. The water, running at a normal pressure of 3–5 bar, is pressed against a semi-permeable membrane, which lets the water pass but retains the substances contained in it (including all the cations and anions, pesticides, bacteria, fungi, and even viruses). The membrane works like the membrane of a living cell, which lets through water but not the salts dissolved in cytoplasm (see Osmotic Pressure, page 28). The water obtained by this procedure is almost fully desalted and contains no organic substances (such as pesticides, bacteria, or viruses). Reverse osmosis is the cheapest method of water preparation. It does not require regeneration (as with ion exchangers), and thus there are no expenses incurred for acids and bases (for neutralization).

The residual water. A small apparatus produces about 100 quarts (liters) of fully desalted, germ- and pesticide-free water each day. However, it also produces about 105 to 130 gallons (400 to 500 liters) of residual water, which flows unused down the drain. Ecologically this is very serious. Moreover, the reverse osmosis equipment should run without interruption, since this increases the life expectancy of the membrane. Although the apparatus can be disconnected, it should never be shut off for more than three weeks; otherwise the membrane dries up and becomes useless. In addition, bacteria and fungi multiply, so that the membrane must be cleaned before it can be used again. Frequent shutdowns shorten the life expectancy of the membrane.

Supplementary equipment. Two filters must be installed to avoid clogging the membrane of the reverse osmosis apparatus and to prevent it from being destroyed. You should install a fine particle filter to trap dirt, rust, sand, and other suspended matter that may be found in the water. Since chlorine could destroy the membrane, an activated charcoal filter must be installed for separating the chlorine. Water may be permitted to enter the apparatus only after this filtering is complete. Provide a spare container to catch the pure water. The residual water can also be caught in another container and used for watering plants, the garden, or for other purposes.

Maintenance. The apparatus can be maintained by regular back-flushing to prevent clogging of the membrane. Larger devices come equipped with reverse flushing mechanisms. The procedure need be done once a month or every other month for about 15 minutes. Washing with citric acid is also possible.

My suggestion: If you live in an area with extremely hard tap water (over 30 dH), you should consider installing an ion exchanger in addition to the reverse osmosis equipment. If the salt concentration of the tap water is too high, the membrane will quickly become clogged. In this case a cation exchanger probably will suffice. The reverse osmosis apparatus will then function primarily as a water purifier.

The Water Environment

Salinization of Water

Water with a very low conductivity (obtained from the ion exchanger or the reverse osmosis apparatus) is not suited for fish breeding. It must now have small amounts of salt added to it—up to about 2 dH for breeding discus fish and cardinal tetras and up to about 6 dH for breeding less sensitive species.

The easiest way to add salt is to replace a small amount of fully desalted water with tap water. The pesticide and nitrate content of the tap water is low enough so that it will not harm the fish.

It is possible to salinize your water with chemicals obtained from a laboratory supply store. In order to harden 26 gallons (100 liters) of water by 1 dH, you need about 1 ounce (30.1 g) calcium sulfate (gypsum), or about 30 mg per quart (liter). Don't use the type of gypsum intended for building purposes. Use only $CaSO_4 \cdot 2H_2O$ from the laboratory supply store.

Spawning involves the whole fish. For a fraction of a second after spawning, one sees the straining of a characin male.

If you also wish to raise the carbonate hardness of your water, add calcium carbonate ($CaCO_3$). It dissolves quickly because it is finely grained. To raise the general and carbonate hardness of 26 gallons (100 liters) of water by 1 dH, you need about 1 dram (.8 g) calcium carbonate.

If the carbonate hardness alone has to be raised, add about $1^3/_4$ drams (3g) sodium hydrogen carbonate ($NaHCO_3$) per 26 gallons (100 liters) of water to raise the hardness by 1 dH.

Many manufacturers of reverse osmosis equipment offer ready-made salt mixtures that resalinize the water after reverse osmosis. Be sure to keep the receipts from the manufacturers of the equipment. For cichlids from Lake Tanganyika and Lake Malawi, which are accustomed to somewhat higher salt concentrations, you can use the ready-made salt mixtures found in pet shops. Since these fish reproduce without problems in hard and medium-hard tap water, preparing water for them is necessary only if they are kept in areas with extremely soft tap water.

Degree of Acidity (pH)

In addition to the hardness of water, the degree of acidity is also important for aquarium occupants. It is expressed in pH units, which reflect the amount of acid dissolved in the water relative to alkali. All natural water contains acids and alkali. If the water contains more acids than alkali, it is acidic; if it contains more alkali than acids, it is alkaline. If the acids and alkali are equal, the water is chemically neutral. *The pH scale* ranges from 0 to 14.
• Neutral water has a pH of 7.
• Water with a pH under 7 is acidic; the lower the pH, the greater the acidity of the water.
• Water with a pH above 7 is alkaline. It becomes more alkaline as the pH increases.

My suggestion: Chemically pure water, such as distilled water, is neutral and has a pH value of 7 as long as it does not come in contact with the air. Carbon dioxide from the air dissolves in the water, forming carbonic acid and dropping the pH to about 5.3.

Even water fresh from the ion exchanger has a low pH. With aeration, however, you can drive off the CO_2 and raise the pH.

Basic Knowledge for the Aquarium Hobbyist

Sharp pH variations harm the fish. Most tropical fish require pH values between 5.8 and 7. Only cichlids from the East African lakes need pH values between 7.5 and 8.5. For most fish the tolerable range of 1.2 pH units seems smaller than it really is, since a change of 1 pH unit indicates a tenfold increase or decrease in the degree of acidity.

• At pH values under 5.5 and above 9, fish are damaged by acids or alkali. The damage is manifested as severe reddening or slimy coating of the skin and corrosion of the gills. The fish scoot around in the tank and rub against the ground or stones. They can die if the pH is not corrected.

• Thus, the pH value must be constantly controlled in the maintenance and breeding tanks. Care must also be taken days later with the transfer of the fish and with periodic partial changes of water in the maintenance and rearing tanks.

• Control of the pH during partial water change is especially important if the aquarium water is saturated with nitrogen compounds (from feeding and fish exreta). When the aquarium is filled with alkaline tap water, the pH climbs from the acidic to the alkaline range, causing ammonium to be converted to poisonous ammonia.

• Under certain conditions, pH changes can result from the actions of plants (such as waterweed and *Vallisneria*), if too little carbon dioxide is dissolved in the water. The pH can rise by one to two units, which means that the water becomes 10 to 100 times more alkaline. In heavily planted tanks you should add CO_2 to the water to avoid such pH variations.

• You can measure the pH with pH indicators or electrical measuring devices (both available at tropical fish stores).

Reducing the pH. For fish from tropical forest waters filtering over peat is often the best solution.

Filter the water for three days before putting in the fish. You can also acidify the water with extracts (see Humic Acids and Peat, page 34). You can also reduce the pH by adding of CO_2 but this requires much experience. Reduction of the pH is necessary for breeding most fish species (for example, characins and discus cichlids).

Long-finned catfish during spawning. The male (right) then takes over the care of the brood.

Raising the pH by raising the carbonate hardness (see page 32) is seldom necessary. A sharp drop in pH can result from defective CO_2 appartus that pumps too much carbon dioxide into the water from careless acidification of very soft water.

My suggestion: Carbonate hardness, pH, and carbon dioxide have a reciprocal relationship in a planted aquarium. Therefore, all three should be controlled constantly.

Humic Acids and Peat

In nature, water is acidified not only by (inorganic) carbonic acid but also by (organic) humic acids, which are formed from dead leaves, deadwood, and other plant material. Humic acids prepare nutrients for water plants; when minerals and trace elements are combined with humic acids, the plants can absorb them better.

Many tropical bodies of water, particularly those in the tropical forest regions, contain much more humic acid than carbonic acid. The highest content of humic acids is found in the black-water rivers of the Amazon region, whose pH can fall below 4, and in some West African rivers. Fish and plants from tropical forest waters are thus used to acidic water and need a supplement of humic acids in the aquarium.

Advantages and disadvantages of humic acids. Humic acids contain tannin, which coats the skin of the fish so that parasitic organisms cannot easily attach themselves. On the other hand, tannin can cause the eggshells to become so hard that the fish larvae cannot break them open at hatching time, and thus die. Therefore, humic acid should be used with caution.

Acidifying with Humic Acids

There are several ways to introduce humic acids into the tank water.

Filtering over peat. Use only unfertilized peat from the pet shop. Peat filtering is the best method of acidifying water for the fish. However, you should test the peat beforehand.

• To test the peat, soften a little amount overnight in distilled water. The next day aerate the specimen with an airstone for about 15 minutes to drive off the carbon dioxide. Next, measure the pH; the water should show a value of 4.5–5.5. If the pH is higher, the peat is unusable.

• To see whether the peat is fertilized or unfertilized, test the same specimen for nitrate, nitrite, and ammonium. Testing kits are available in tropical fish stores. If you detect traces of these substances in the water, you should not use the peat.

If you have good, unfertilized peat, you can attach it to the filter (see page 16).

Acidifying with peat extracts. Using the dosage instructions of the manufacturer will provide the proper amount of peat extract in the aquarium water.

Acidifying with oak bark or spruce cones. Oak bark or spruce cones are boiled in distilled water to obtain a standard solution. Test this solution to see what amount of it changes the pH value of a given volume of water by a specific amount. Once you have determined the proper value, you can proceed without worry. But since the tannin content of the bark and cones varies according to the location of the trees as well as from year to year, every freshly prepared standard solution must be tested. If you fail to determine the strength of the solution, you can add excess tannic acid and lower the pH too much.

My suggestion: Don't acidify with sulfuric or nitric acid. The addition of strong inorganic acids can cause the pH to drop very rapidly into ranges fatal to fish. This is especially true of soft water.

Nitrogen Compounds

Nitrogen is a component of proteins which comprise the bulk of organic matter in living organisms. Hardly any nitrogen compounds are found in clean natural waters. The aquarium, however, is always overpopulated compared with comparable volume of water in nature. Therefore, it contains many decoposition products originating from food particles, decayed plant matter, dead bacteria, slugs, and fish. These materials can easily reach a dangerous concentration. Nitrogen compounds can be measured and controlled with liquid indicators or with testing strips (both of which are available in specialty stores).

Ammonia and Ammonium

Ammonia is a powerful poison. Ammonium, on the other hand, is almost non-toxic. Which of these substances is formed in water depends on the pH.

The Water Environment

Ammonium develops in acidic water and ammonia in alkaline water.

In lightly acidic aquarium water the fish are not in danger of ammonia poisoning. In alkaline water, however, ammonium is converted to the poisonous ammonia.

Advice for the aquarium hobbyist:
• Control the pH of the water constantly.
• Should you—for whatever reason—have neglected your aquarium for months, and your fish wallow in waste, they are not in danger of ammonia poisoning as long as the pH remains in the acidic range.
• Be careful, however, when you clean a very dirty aquarium and undertake a partial water change. If the tap water is strongly alkaline, the pH will rise and the ammonium will change to ammonia, which will poison the fish.
• To clean a very dirty aquarium, it is recommended that you exchange three-quarters or four-fifths of the tank water for fresh water. This will lower the ammonia concentration to such an extent that the fish will no longer be endangered.
• Water plants absorb ammonium as a nutrient. You can therefore place them in the aquarium as water purifiers. The waterweed is particularly effective in this.

Perch from the East African lakes, which live in alkaline water, are constantly threatened by ammonia poisoning in dirty aquariums. These fish are voracious eaters and—for the most part—are kept in unplanted aquariums, since many of them eat plants. Therefore, install an especially powerful filter for these fish, and change the water more often than with other fish.
• In well cared for aquariums, the concentration of ammonium is about a fraction of a grain per quart (0.5 mg per liter). This is perfectly safe for the fish. Higher values are harmless as long as the pH remains in the acidic or weakly alkaline range (never more than a pH of 8).
• If ammonia builds up to a value of 0.2 to 0.6 mg per liter, the fish will begin to gasp for air. It is easy to confuse ammonia poisoning with lack of oxygen. Therefore, always remember to consider both possibilities.

Nitrates and Nitrites
Ammonia and ammonium are converted by filter bacteria (*Nitrosomonas*) to highly poisonous nitrites, which, in turn, are converted (by *Nitrobacter* bacteria) to relatively nonpoisonous nitrates. This "bacterial nitrification" requires a lot of oxygen.

The dangers of oxygen deprivation:
• When the oxygen concentration of the water is low, the bacteria work too slowly or not at all. The filter may then remain at the nitrite stage for too long, and the fish can perish from nitrite poisoning.
• If the water contains large amounts of nitrates, the entire reaction can run in reverse. Thus nitrates are converted to nitrites, which, in turn, are converted to ammonium and ammonia.

Important Information for the Aquarium Hobbyist
• Nitrite poisoning has the same effect on fish as ammonia poisoning, lack of oxygen, or an excess of CO_2. The fish dash around the tank, gasp for air near the surface, and suffocate if the water problem is not corrected. The nitrite content of the water should not rise above 0.2 mg per quart (liter); at concentrations of over 0.5 mg many fish start gasping for air.
• Fish tolerate nitrates better than nitrites. If possible the aquarium water should not contain more than 20 mg of nitrates per quart (liter). Since tap water can contain up to 50 mg per liter, obviously the aquarium water will contain more than 20 mg per quart (liter). Fish cannot tolerate more than 150 to 200 mg per quart (liter).
• What applies to ammonium and ammonia also applies to nitrates and nitrites. Change the water regularly and measure its nitrogen content in order to keep the nitrogen compounds to a minimum.
• Swamp and land plants absorb nitrates. Among the swamp plants, *Hygrophila* species have shown themselves to be particularly useful in water purification. Even land plants can be put into the tank as nitrate consumers. Place a philodendron (*Monstera deliciosa*) close to the aquarium and let a few aerial roots grow inside the tank. They will soon branch out within the tank and absorb the nitrates.

The Water Environment

- There are also small ion exchangers that remove nitrates from the water. However, they exchange nitrate ions for chloride ions, and many fish cannot tolerate this.
- Tap water containing large amounts of nitrates can be made usable by reverse osmosis (see page 31).
- If you have large tanks or a large breeding setup, you would be best served by a large filtering system, which can convert nitrates to nitrogen. Such systems are very expensive. You can check it out in your tropical fish store, or you can even build one of these large filters yourself. You'll find instructions in the aquarium magazines.
- If the concentration of ammonia, ammonium, and nitrates increase sharply after a water change, then the aquarium is overpopulated or the filter is too small.
- A consistently high nitrite content indicates the same thing. Frequently nitrites are found in newly installed tanks in which the filter has not run long enough and there are not enough bacteria to convert the nitrites present.

What You Should Know for Breeding
- Eggs and fry are much more sensitive to nitrogen compounds than adult fish. High concentrations of ammonia and nitrates hinder the growth of the fry noticeably and make them susceptible to diseases.
- Many fish in rearing tanks are abundantly fed, which produces large amounts of nitrogen decomposition products. Therefore, change about half the water daily and remove excess food. Following this procedure will visibly increase your success in breeding.
- In breeding aquariums you can remove nitrates with *Monstera* roots.
- When the fry of mouthbreeding fish have devoured their yolk sacs and are ready for feeding, attach a large external filter (in which sufficient bacterial cultures have formed) to the aquarium tank.
- In spawning tanks avoid feeding at all, or feed only once with washed white worms (Enchytraen see page 42). This will help to avoid unncessary soiling.

Phosphates

Animals need phosphates for building their skeleton, while plants require them for their metabolism. Aquarium water can contain large amounts of phosphates, which can be absorbed from food particles or added with tap water during water changes. Drinking water can contain up to 1.6 mg of phosphates per quart (liter).
Ideally the aquarium water should not contain more than 0.5 mg of phosphates per quart (liter) of water. You can measure the phosphate content with a liquid indicator obtained commercially.
You can lower the phosphate content through reverse osmosis (see page 31) or by full desalting with an ion exchanger (see page 29).

Chlorine

Tap water sometimes contains chlorine as a disinfectant. It can usually be detected by its strong odor. Chlorine is a powerful poison that kills the fish by gill corrosion.
You can measure the chlorine content with commercially available liquid indicators. Under no circumstances should the aquarium water contain more than 0.1 mg chlorine per quart (liter) of water. To remove the chlorine collect the chlorinated water in large containers and let it stand for a few hours, stirring the water several times each hour. This will cause the chlorine to evaporate. It can also be filtered out by activated charcoal (see page 16).

South American ground-spawning killifish. Fish of the pearl-fish species *Cynolebias viarius* are ground plungers. Thus the male (larger) and the female (front) plunge right into the soft ground and spawn there together.

36

Copper

Copper can get into the tap water from newly installed water pipes or from freshly cleaned boilers. In hard water it is precipitated as an alkaline copper salt, but not in soft water. Copper is a strong poison for all water organisms. In hard water fish tolerate up to 2 mg copper for per quart (liter), in soft water only 0.01 mg. Copper is measured with a liquid indicator. To remove copper from the aquarium, change the water. But if your tap water contains copper you can remove it by using methods that will precipitate the copper and other heavy metals or by reverse osmosis (see page 31).

Measuring and Testing Tools

Various reagents and indicators, and instruments for testing water can be obtained in tropical fish or pet shops.

Liquid color indicators are available for most tests. You add them to a water sample until a color change is obtained. The number of drops or the color intensity is then determined and compared with the tables or color charts that are provided.

Indicator strips are used for some tests. One dips them into the water specimen and compares the color change with the test charts.

Small water testing kits that have all the important test reagents are available from pet shops and specialty stores. They are also offered by the environmental protection agency Greenpeace.

Electrical measuring instruments are more expensive initially. However, if you breed often and perform many water tests, they are cheaper in the long run.

Permanently installed electronic measuring and testing equipment is available for larger tanks as well as for larger breeding setups. Such devices measure everything from salt concentration to pH, hardness, temperature, oxygen and CO_2 levels, nitrogen content, and so on. Many devices also regulate the supply of fresh water, regeneration of ion exchangers, and so on.

African ground-spawning killifish. Mating Beira nothobranch (*Nothobranchius melanospilus*) male drapes his wide dorsal fin around the female and presses her partly into the soft ground. They spawn side by side. When they dig themselves out, the eggs are pressed still more deeply into the ground.

Three armored catfish males vie for a female ready to spawn. Success belongs to him who manages to get in front of the female crosswise (in a T-formation). Here one has succeeded. The female will deposit a few eggs in her fin pocket, while the male, with a movement of his tail fin, will push his sperm in the direction of the eggs.

Disinfecting Water in the Breeding Tank

Treatment with ozone or ultraviolet light can make
breeding water relatively germfree.
*Ozone (O$_3$) for fighting bacteria, infusorians, fungi,
and viruses.* Ozonization is not a simple method
and is somewhat risky. Inform yourself thoroughly
in the tropical fish stores and by consulting with
other hobbyists before you get involved with it.
Ozone works as a strong oxidizing agent, killing
small organisms such as bacteria, infusorians,
fungi, and viruses. It must not reach too high a
level or it can harm the fishes' gills.
In planted aquariums it is best not to use ozonization, as it oxidizes plant nutrients. Ozone is most
frequently used in small unplanted aquariums in
which large broods are raised.
Ultraviolet light. Ultraviolet (UV) light is rich in
energy and can be used to inhibit the growth of
unwanted small organisms such as bacteria. It is
especially suited for rearing tanks, which are
heavily populated with sensitive fry or for breeding
tanks with species such as the penguin fish
(Thayeria boelkei), which produce large amounts
of sperm.
You need a UV lamp specially manufactured for
the aquarium hobbyist, which is installed in the
outside filter of a motor driven unit. The filter
water flows directly past the lamp and thus
becomes disinfected. Find out what lamp output (in
watts) you need for your breeding tanks and filter.
Breeding suggestion: Never place a UV lamp in
front of the breeding tank, as this will harm the fish
and their brood.

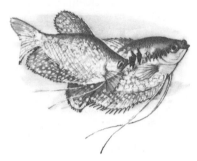

Mating Pearl Gouramis. The partners prod each
gently in the flanks with their mouths.

Types of Food and Feeding

Vitamins and roughage keep breeding fish from getting too fat. Fatty degeneration harms the functioning of all the internal organs, especially those of the gonads. Fattened fish often suffer from difficulty in spawning. On the other hand, fish should not be too thin prior to spawning, otherwise egg production strains them so that they quickly become exhausted and die young.

Rice fish (killifish) female with egg clusters. After spawning the fertilized eggs remain in the anal region for a while before they are laid.

Dry Food

Dry food contains everything that fish need: protein, carbohydrates, vitamins, minerals, and roughage. This food is available as food flakes, which come in different sizes, and as food tablets, which are used for bottom feeders.

There is no single food for breeding fish. Although dry food is convenient to use, your fish should not be fed dry food exclusively. Most of the fastidious species (such as killifish, characins and catfish) usually will not begin to spawn unless they receive a variety of live food. Fish in the wild prefer to feed on insect larvae, small crustaceans, and an occasional worm. Since these creatures feed on algae and protozoa, they are far richer in vitamins and minerals than the best dry food. In addition, fish must hunt for live food, which provides them with exercise and keeps them in shape.

Live Food

Live food is available from tropical fish stores and pet shops. It can also be obtained from home garden pools or caught in clean ponds in your area.

Worms
Tubifex, a red mud worm, can be obtained throughout the year in any good pet shop. Unfortunately, *Tubifex* worms are often contaminated with heavy metals and other poisons that can cause severe illness in aquarium fish. Under no circumstances should *Tubifex* worms be fed to delicate fish (such as discus fish). Feed them to hardier species only when you cannot get any other live food.

If you use *Tubifex* as food, soak the worms thoroughly for a few days prior to using them. Put the *Tubifex* clusters in a container with flowing water; in stagnant water the worms will die in a few hours. Once a day lift up the cluster of worms and rinse away the dirt that has accumulated. After about three days, the *Tubifex* can be fed in small portions. They are not rich in vitamins. Shortly before feeding add a few drops of a multivitamin preparation to the water. The *Tubifex* will then absorb some of the vitamin product.

Earthworms can be bought in bait shops or dug up in your yard or garden. Since they are very nutritious, you can feed them to the fish exclusively for a long time without the fish showing any signs of deficiency. Earthworms provide good nourishment for large cichlids, catfish, and other carnivorous fish. The red earthworm (*Lumbricus rubellus*) is a favorite of most of these fish. Before using earthworms as food, you should keep them for a few days in darkened crates with damp toilet paper (unbleached, uncolored), so that they will shed their outer mucous covering and lose the earth that adheres to their skin.

Types of Food and Feeding

Earthworms can be bred in a compost heap or in nourishing, loose earth mixed with sawdust. They should multiply when fed a mixture of grass and garden clippings.

White worms such as *Enchytraeus albus* and *Enchytraeus buchholtzi* are relatives of *Tubifex* and earthworms. After you purchase these (for use as starter cultures), place them in very large plastic or styrofoam containers. These containers must be thoroughly washed, so that they do not smell of plastic or release chemicals.

Fill the containers about 2 inches (5 cm) high with damp peat that has been softened for a few days in water and then squeezed dry and finely ground. The containers must have tiny air holes and remain dark.

Enchytraeus albus worms multiply at 50 to 59°F (10 to 15°C) on a diet of oatmeal, brown bread, and powdered milk at a ratio of 1:5.

Enchytraeus buchholtzi worms multiply at 68 to 77°F (20 to 25°C) on a diet of oatmeal, brown bread, and powdered milk at a ratio of 3:3:1. All the ingredients are mixed, put on the damp, loose peat surface, and gently tamped down. The peat is sprayed with water, and the containers are covered with thin material such as gauze or dishcloth. Warning: If there is too little air during breeding, the food will begin to ferment and get so hot that the worms will crawl out of the containers. Mold can also form. If the worms are afflicted with mites, they must be washed and put in fresh peat. A breeding setup should be replaced every two months by a new colony.

To use the worms as food; press a glass pane gently to the peat surface. The worms will stick to the glass pane; they can then be washed off and used as food. Do not overfeed fish with these worms because they have a high fat content.

Insect Larvae

Red midge larvae, (larvae of the midge *Chironomus*) somtimes are available in tropical fish stores in winter. They should be used with caution because they have been shown to cause frequent indigestion.

Since red midge larvae have tough skins, you should chop them up before feeding them to small fish and fry. They can chew through the intestine and stomach walls of these fish if they are still alive. Feed them only in small portions. Larvae that are not eaten immediately sink to the bottom, where they burrow into the ground-feeding fish such as catfish, loaches, larger carp, and cichlids. These larvae can be stored in shallow pans with cold water. Before feeding them to your fish, pour the larvae and water into a strainer and rinse well. On hot days replace the water several times, or the larvae will die. Larger amounts can be placed in damp egg cartons and preserved in the refrigerator. But be careful—they don't smell good!

White midge larvae, the larvae of the midge *Corethra*, are not really transparent. They normally live only in very clean bodies of water and are seldom available in stores. These creatures are accustomed to cold and die quickly in the warm water of the tropical aquarium. Therefore, use them as food only in small, limited portions.

Preserve white midge larvae in cold water in shallow containers. Store in a cool room or in a container aerated with an airstone.

Black gnat larvae are the larvae of various biting gnats (*Culex*). They can be found in the summer in standing bodies of water. You can find large quantities of black gnat larvae in flooded meadows, sunny pools, and in the flat shore areas of ponds and seas.

Black gnat larvae are among the best and most important food sources. They are so rich in vitamins, minerals, and protein that they stimulate most fish to spawn. Black gnat larvae are especially good for surface fish such as live-bearing and egg-laying toothed carp, labyrinth fish, young butterfly fish, and many others. Be careful that you don't give more of these larvae than the fish can eat at one time, because the larvae can develop into biting gnats.

You can store small amounts of live larvae in cold water, in shallow and wide containers that provide enough area for the larvae to obtain air at the surface.You can also freeze the larvae (see page 44).

Types of Food and Feeding

Insects

Many female fish spawn better if they are also fed insects. This is especially true for surface fish, which in the wild live almost exclusively on insects (for example, butterfly fish). You can have fertilized eggs of various insect species sent to you. *Small and large fruit flies (Drosophila melanogaster* and *Drosophila hydei*), also called vinegar flies, come in both winged and unwinged breeding forms. The unwinged ones are better suited for aquarial fish.

Paradise fish pair under foam nest. The male (front) has invested much time and energy in the building of the foam nest.

Fruit flies can be bred in flasks, obtained from laboratory supply stores, or in glass containers. Maintain a temperature of 68 to 77°F (20 to 25°C). Prepare a mash consisting of oat flakes, oatmeal, and wheat bran at a ratio of 1:1:1 with a teaspoon of powdered milk. Whip this into a thick mixture with white wine and some water. A drop of antimold powder will prevent the mixture from becoming moldy.

Place the mash into the flasks to a height of about 1 inch (3 cm). Add a loose coil of filter paper containing the fertilized fruit fly eggs. Cover the jars with a piece of gauze fastened with a rubber band. If the food dries out, dampen it with water. If it gets moldy or begins to ferment, put the flies in a fresh jar with new mash.

To use the fruit flies as food; rotate the flask and carefully shake the desired amount of flies into a plastic bag; empty the bag into the aquarium. Fruit flies are suitable mainly for surface fish under 3 inches (8 cm) in length; larger fish are not sated with these small flies.

Common house flies (Musca domestica) are suitable for larger fish. Flightless, blind varieties are available in specialty stores. Since breeding common house flies generates very unpleasant odors, the aquarium hobbyist should not attempt it. *Moths.* Large moths, such as *Galleria mellonella,* and small ones, such as *Achroea grisella* and *Plodia interpunctella*, are desirable food for larger fish.

Keep the moths in well ventilated jars covered with a thick layer of gauze to prevent them from escaping when they emerge from the eggs. Put pieces of honeycomb in the jars for large moths. For smaller moths use a mixture of honey, glycerin, vitamins, oat flakes, oatmeal, wheat bran, grits and yeast.

Small Crustaceans

Small crayfish include water fleas of the genera *Daphnia, Cyclops, Diaptomus,* and *Bosmina. Daphnia* are caught in the summer in ponds and pools. They are a wonderful supplement for dry food but are not nourishing enough as a single source of food. *Cyclops* are found more rarely than *Daphnia* because they need clean water.

You can store small amounts of *Daphnia* in a container with well aerated water (use an airstone). If you have large amounts, it is better to freeze them (see below).

To breed *Daphnia*: place them in about 5 to 50 quarts (liters) of water, gently aerate the water with an airstone, and gradually siphon it off. Feed the *Daphnia* with a solution of baker's yeast and water a few drops at a time just until the water turns cloudy but not milky. Feed the *Daphnia* again only when they have consumed all the yeast, and the water becomes clear.

To use the *Daphnia* as food siphon off the contents of the breeding jar into a strainer. The *Daphnia* will remain in the strainer.

My suggestion: Don't rinse out the empty breeding jar. Just refill it with fresh water. The remaining *Daphnia* will form a new breeding group.

Frozen Food

You can freeze live food yourself or buy it frozen.

Freezing Live Food
Live food can be frozen just as easily as perishable groceries. The only exception is worms, especially *Tubifex*, which become mushy when thawed.
Here's how it's done. One method is to freeze small portions of live food in ice cube trays. Or you can spread the live food in layers about 2mm thick on plastic or aluminum foil and cover tightly with another sheet of aluminum foil. You thus get thin sheets from which you can break off pieces as you need them.
Warning. Always put live food in the freezer (not in the refrigerator). This ensures that the food will retain its nutritional value over an extended period.

Commerically Available Frozen Live Food
You can often buy frozen live food at a local pet shop. In addition to midge larvae and *Daphnia* you may find ocean animals such as mussels, fish roe, *Artemia* (brine shrimp), and Mysis shrimp.
Mysis, the wonder food. An occasional diet of Mysis stimulates fish to spawn. With fish that have already begun to spawn you can accelerate the process by feeding them Mysis exclusively for a few days. Unfortunately, freshwater fish do not tolerate too much of this salt-rich diet. For long-term feeding give it as a food supplement no more than twice a week.

Proper Feeding of Frozen Food
Thaw the frozen food completely, otherwise the fish can suffer severe and possibly fatal indigestion.
• Let the frozen food lie at room temperature until it is soft.
• Do not refreeze thawed food.
• If you thaw too much food, discard the rest. Bacteria and toxins can form very easily—and they are deadly to the fish.

Provide Every Species of Fish with the Right Food
Amateur breeders who breed fish only occasionally do not need a whole battery of live food animals. For small tropical fish (such as characins, barbs, live-young bearing toothed carp, and labyrinth fish) small live food animals (such as midge larvae and *Daphnia*) and dry food flakes are sufficient. Fish with more demanding needs (such as catfish, egg-laying toothed carp, many cichlids, and large labyrinth fish) are content with white worms (*Enchytraeus albus* or *Enchytraeus buchholzi*), which you can collect yourself in two or three containers. Egg-laying toothed carp can be given a supplement of small fruit flies. Large fish (such as cichlids and catfish) require larger live food such as earthworms, mealworms, or moth larvae. Insect-eating surface fish (such as butterfly fish) can be given crickets and cockroaches in addition to live moths. You can obtain live mealworms, crickets, and cockroaches in pet shops. If you would like to breed these animals yourself, you will need a special room in which no harm is done if a few food animals escape from their containers.

Substitutes for Live Food

As a substitute for live food you can use freshwater or saltwater fish or animal meat such as finely chopped beef liver. Fish meat is very suitable for most fish. Animal meat, however, harms their digestion. It should be offered only rarely and in very small quantities. Any food not consumed within five minutes should immediately be removed from the water. Otherwise it will decompose and spoil the water.

Plant Food

In their natural habitat no fish live exclusively on animal or plant food.

Meat eaters (carnivores, such as cichlids and labyrinth fish), when eating fish, crabs, and insects, also devour the intestines of their prey, which contain green algae and other plants. Therefore, these fish need plant food as an occasional supplement to their diet.

Plant eaters (herbivores, such as sucker-mouth armored catfish) may also eat baby crabs and worms that are found among the algae or on plant leaves. You can offer them worms, larvae, and dry food tablets.

Ancistrus male caring for eggs. Plant food is essential for the breeding of *Ancistrus* species.

Types of Plant Food

Algae grow in every aquarium but for the most part do not meet the needs of fish. All herbivorous fish or those that eat plants as a part of their diet (such as cichlids from Lakes Tanganyika and Malawi) are especially fond of dry vegetable flakes.

Lettuce is often recommended as a food for herbivorous fish. It has been found, however, that fish stopped spawning if they were fed commercially grown lettuce that had been treated with chemicals. They did not resume spawning until several weeks after the lettuce was removed from their diet. Therefore, feed your fish only lettuce that has been raised organically and contains no chemicals or additives.

Spinach can be used fresh (when it's new) or thawed (after freezing). It's a favorite food, but many fish must get accustomed to it slowly.

Wild plants such as dandelions greens and chickweed can also be used to feed fish after they become accustomed to them.

Surplus water plants from other aquariums, which occasionally become available when pruning and planting, can be prepared as food for plant eaters. Slugs and other animals that live on the plants are also eaten. Large cichlids enjoy duckweeds.

How to Feed

Lettuce, spinach, and wild plant greens should be soaked for a short time before feeding so that they become soft. Frozen spinach need only be thawed.

How Often and How Much to Feed

Breeding fish are not fed more often than other fish in the community aquarium. However, they receive live food, which is richer in nutrients and can thus provide them with additional vitamins and iodine. If you purchase fry that you intend to use later for breeding, do not keep them in the company of larger or more lively fish. Such fish can deprive the fry of food.

Reproductive Biology and Fish Behavior

The Evolutionary Adaptation of Fish

Fish constantly adapt to their environment. Environmental factors affect their physical characteristics as well as their reproductive and social behavior. Only those characteristics that help the fish survive and reproduce will be passed on to future generations. Every species, therefore, develops its own strategies of reproduction. Some interesting and different strategies can be observed even in aquarium fish.

Unisexual Fish

Most fish are unisexual, that is, they are either male or female. Females produce eggs in the ovaries, and males produce sperm in the testes. The sexual organs are located in pairs on both sides of the vertebral column. In some fish (for example, live-bearing toothed carp), the paired ovaries have merged into a single pouch. The ovaries are connected to the oviduct, and the testes to the spermatic duct. Both ducts empty into the genital papilla behind the anus.

Hermaphroditic Fish

Hermaphroditic fish were formerly regarded as rare, but the more research in this area has progressed, the more hermaphroditic species have been found. Hermaphroditic fish can be divided into two categories:
• Gradual hermaphrodites are fish that change their sex in the course of their life, but are either male or female at any single stage.
• Simultaneous hermaphrodites can function as males and females at the same time (they possess both male and female organs).
• Hermaphroditic fish are found primarily in the ocean. Which fish becomes a male and which a female depends mainly on its rank. With most species, dominant fish develop into males and subordinate fish into females.

Reproductive Strategies of Unisexual Fish

Fish can be classified according to their reproductive strategies—those that lay eggs and those that bear living young.

Pike-top minnow (carp) prior to mating. The male has already moved his gonopodium toward the front of his body.

Egg-laying Fish

The fish of this group are differentiated according to size, the type and quantity of their eggs, and the amount of care they provide for their brood.
Useful knowledge about eggs. Fish eggs usually are small (between 1.5 and 3 mm on the average) and round. There are also species with egg-shaped, very large eggs (over 7 mm in length) as, for example, most of the mouth-breeding cichlids. Most fish eggs are heavier than water and sink to the bottom. Many are sticky and cling to plants or other structures. Others, such as the eggs of the rainbow fish (*Melanotaeniidae*) have sticky threads with which they attach themselves. The eggs of many armored catfish (*Loricariidae*) cling together

in a thick clump, which the tending male carries around in his mouth. Many fish species, such as the kissing gourami (*Helostoma temmincki*) and spiny eels (*Mastacembelidae*), lay eggs capable of floating; they contain oil drops that give them buoyancy in the water.

Schooling fish. Many fish, mostly smaller species (for example, many characins and carp) do not pair off in the wild but spawn in schools, often after very long spawning trips to a designated body of water. They lay large numbers of eggs, which either float and drift away, or they sink and attach themselves to plants or to the bottom. Since the female carries a large number of eggs in a limited space, each egg is small and contains little yolk. These fish do not care for their brood. The large number of eggs that they lay ensures that some of the eggs will survive loss by predators. Schooling fish often live in open waters without opportunity for cover (oceans, large freshwater seas, large rivers) where caring for the brood is not feasible.

Territorial fish. Fish species (such as cichlids and labyrinth fish) that live in waters with many hiding places occupy territories, prepare spawning areas, or build nests. In many of these species the males and females pair off for the rearing of a brood and even for the entire reproductive period. In other species one male mates with many females, forming a harem. In some species the males live together in colonies and mate with females that wander from one spawning place to another, having their eggs fertilized by different males. In general, territorial fish care for their brood. Among other things, the egg size depends on the availability of food in the water. Species from waters with abundant microflora and microfauna (algae, bacteria, infusorians, rotifers, and so on) generally have large spawns, in which the individual eggs are just as small and poor in yolk as in free-spawning fish. Other species—especially those from waters with a poor food supply—lay few eggs but these are large eggs that are rich in yolk.

Other reproductive strategies.

• Some fish entrust the protection and the rearing of their young to other species. The cuckoo catfish

(*Synodontis petricola*), for example, lets its eggs be cared for by mouthbreeding cichlids.

• Other fish can protect fertilized eggs in their bodies until the emergence of the young. Females of some catfish varieties (*Aspredinidae*) carry the spawn in their stomachs. Mouthbreeding cichlids and labyrinth fish protect the eggs in their mouths.

• The eggs of some egg-laying fish are fertilized internally. Females are first impregnated by the males and then lay their eggs alone. Examples are American Characins of the subfamily *Glandulocaudinae* and catfish of the family *Auchenipteridae*.

Fish that Bear Living Young

In live-bearing fish the eggs are fertilized internally in the female. When mating, the male transmits the spermatozoa (in the form of a sperm packet) by means of a mating organ, which in most species has developed from the anal fin. In live-bearing toothed carp (*Poeciliidae*) the modified anal fin is called the gonopodium (see photo, page 55). Live-bearing species are classified as ovoviviparous and viviparous.

With ovoviviporous species the eggs develop inside the mother's body without the mother providing additional nourishment to the embryos. The young develop inside the eggs and absorb food from the yolk. The eggshell breaks when the young are born. An exception is the midget live bearer (*Heterandria formosa*), in which a type of placenta similar to that of mammals has developed. In viviparous fish the mother nourishes the young in her body by secreting various substances. The young of the highland carp (*Goodeidae*), the closest relatives of the live-bearing toothed carp, are nourished by a type of "umbilical cord" directly from the mother's circulating blood. Highland carp young are maintained and reared like live-bearing toothed carp (see page 100).

Bearing living young offers many advantages for the offspring:

• The eggs and the young are protected from all predators that are too small to attack the mother herself.

• The young cannot perish in an unfavorable

environment (for instance, lack of oxygen or great heat) as long as the mother herself survives.
• A solitary pregnant female can establish a new population in a hitherto unpopulated environment.
• After an environmental catastrophe, a surviving pregnant female can resettle in the former environment.
• In many live-bearing fish (for example, live-bearing toothed carp) one mating is sufficient for several broods, since the sperm can be stored in the folds of the fallopian tube wall. This raises the chances of survival of the species.

Brood Care

Brood-tending fish have fewer young than those that do not tend their brood (free spawners), but these young are bigger and stronger than those of free spawners. They have better chances of survival because they are protected from predators and are brought up in an atmosphere that is favorable for their development. The eggs of free spawners, on the other hand, are often left to drift in a life-threatening environment. Brood care demands a considerable expenditure of time and energy and, as a rule, shortens the life of the parents.
Fish that care for their young in a life-threatening environment (oxygen-poor water, predators) have often developed brood-tending strategies for the survival of their young that demand a high expenditure of energy.
Foam nests are built by the males of many species of labyrinth fish (see page 126 and photos page 8 and 101) and of callichthyd catfish (*Callichthyidae;* see page 86). The adult fish, which sometimes live in very warm, oxygen-poor waters, possess accessory breathing organs with which they can take in atmospheric air. Their young do not have such organs.
The males work all day on their foam nests before spawning. They gulp in air, cover it with saliva, and spit out bubbles toward the water surface. There the bubbles cling fast to each other and to floating plants. Many species also include plants in

their nests. Foam nests can be quite big—those of the armored catfish raise about 1¹/₄ inches (3 cm) above the water surface.
Even after spawning the male must constantly build up the foam nest, collect the eggs and young that have fallen out, and spit them back into the nest. This requires much effort and energy, but the foam nest is an especially effective means of rearing the young in oxygen-poor water.
Fish eggs—and embryos in particular—require oxygen; lack of oxygen causes deformity (see page 65). The oxygen content in a foam nest is much higher than in the surrounding water; moreover, it is cooler in the nest. The foam may even impede the development of bacteria, so that the young are protected from diseases and parasites. Only when they are prepared for the living conditions of their native waters do they leave the nest.
Skin mucus for nourishment of the young is produced by discus cichlids (*Symphysodon aequifasciatus*) and other cichlids. Mucus cells in the skin of the parent fish become enlarged and produce great quantities of whittish, cloudy mucus. The young feed on it when they become free-swimming (see photo on inside front cover).
Discus fish live in tropical forest water that is strongly acidic and rich in tannin. This water is poor in microorganisms such as bacteria, infusoria, and algae, which small fry normally feed on. The body mucus is a substitute for these microorganisms.
The citron cichlids (*Cichlasoma citrinellum*) from Central America also secretes mucus as food for its young. It spawns in overly populated shallow water areas of large lakes in which each pair can secure at most 2 square yards (meters) for rearing over 1000 young. The skin mucus of the parents provides sufficient nourishment for the young.
Mouth care of the brood has developed independently in many fish species (see photos on page 73 and on the inside and outside back covers).
Mobility of the brood is an important factor in protection of the young, since it enables them to escape from predators. The tending parent (mostly the female) can survive with little or no food for days or weeks.

Reproductive Biology and Fish Behavior

Females of the highly specialized mouthbreeders from the East African lakes can hold their young in their mouths for up to a month. They grow very thin during this period and need some time to recuperate afterward. The young in the mouth of the mother are nourished by their large yolk sacs. The yolk sacs are not consumed until the fry are well developed and ready to be released from the mouth.

Young discus fish at "pasture." The mucus secreted from the parent's skin replaces the meager plankton nourishment of the native habitat.

Even after the offspring leave the mouth some mouthbreeding species defend them ferociously against predators. Mouthbreeding females from the East African lakes attack fish that are more than twice their size and manage to drive them away. The young sink to the ground among the pebbles and barely move until the mother returns and takes them back into her mouth (see photo on page 56).

Additional Strategies to Increase Breeding Success

Fish can also increase their reproductive success by exploiting the time and energy of other individuals or species for rearing their young and use the energy thus saved to produce more offspring.

Egg Substitution
The cuckoo catfish (*Synodontis peticola*) from Lake Tanganyika eats the eggs of mouthbreeding cichlid females while they are spawning and substitutes her own eggs, which the cichlids raise as their own offspring (see page 94).

Egg Decoys
The males of many East African mouthbreeding cichlids (such as the genera *Haplochromis, Pseudotropheus, Melanochromis,* and *Aulonocara*) have large, round yellow-orange spots on their anal fin that resemble the eggs of these species in size and color. In this way the males "seduce" the females to reproduce (see illustration on page 50). These mouthbreeders do not form pairs; the partners come together only to spawn.
The males occupy territories, select a spawning area, and mate with females that swim past. A mating male swims up to the female, stops short before her, and shakes violently. He thus spreads his anal fin with its "eggs" toward her. He then leads the female to the spawning area, stopping a few times along the way and again showing her his "eggs." Often he also releases an odorous material and even some sperm, which stimulates the female. If the female is ready to spawn, she follows the male to the spawning areas, where the male vibrates on his side and again releases sperm. The female circles around the male and lays one or more eggs, which she immediately takes in her mouth. She tries to gather up the "eggs" from the anal fin of the male, thereby sucking in the sperm that the male releases. Apparently, the female mistakes the fake eggs for real ones, thus allowing the eggs in her mouth to be fertilized by the sperm of the male.

Reproductive Biology and Fish Behavior

Mating of Mouthbreeding Haplochromis cichlids. The male spreads his anal fin, which is covered with egg spots, and releases sperm. The female, which is attracted to the egg spots, sucks in the sperm and thus fertilizes the eggs in her mouth.

There is another breeding success "secret" at the root of this behavior. The sperm of these mouthbreeders are capable of living in the water for more than half an hour; thus the eggs could be fertilized in the spawning area. Therefore, there must be another reason for the female to take the eggs and sperm into her mouth. The males of many mouthbreeders—especially those that have the largest and most splendid "eggs"—live in colonies. Wind, water currents, and the males' territorial battles spread the sperm into neighboring spawning areas. Each spawning area thus contains not only the sperm of the owner, who has invested time and energy in territory building, but also those of his rivals. These sperm decrease the reproductive success of the territory builder. When the male exhibits beautiful, large "eggs," he attracts the female to his anal fin and thus to his genitals. The female then takes his sperm into her mouth, and the eggs are fertilized by the proper male.

The female also benefits from this behavior. Offspring descended from a father strong enough to best his rivals and establish a territory are likely to inherit his strength and have a good chance at reproduction.

Seed Stealing

Young and weak cichlid males that cannot establish a territory (so-called satellite males), ensure for themselves a small chance at reproductive success by approaching dominant male territory owners in female coloration and following them when they mate. The satellite males pretend to lay eggs but actually deposit their sperm, which become part of the general sperm pool. Without territory and a spawning place, such males could never attract a female and would be unable to reproduce. This behavior is found not only in East African mouthbreeders, but has also been observed in the wild with North American sun perch (*Centrarchidae*) and in the aquarium with different South American dwarf cichlids of the genus *Apistogramma*.

Exploitation of One's Own Partner

Reproduction success can also be increased at the expense of the sexual partner. This is found in cichlids that engage in prolonged pair bonding. Males and females of the Indian cichlids (*Etroplus maculatus*), for example, share in the care of the eggs and larvae. They take turns in guarding the eggs, cleaning the brood, and fanning fresh water to the eggs and later to the emerged larvae. The brood-tending partner thereby expends much energy and cannot eat. The other partner, who patrols the territorial boundaries, has time to eat and does not work very hard.

Observation of aquarium fish has shown that the weaker partner—whether male or female—often spends more time tending the brood, while the stronger one stays in the territory and eats especially often at feeding time. The stronger partner also nudges the weaker one toward the brood when the weaker partner stops tending. The stronger fish thus expends less energy on brood care and is capable of starting a new brood earlier.

Reproductive Biology and Fish Behavior

In addition, a fish that stays at the territorial boundries has more opportunities to mate with other fish in the area.

In general, males are more inclined to leave their partners and offspring and begin a new brood with another female. Females must invest much more energy in the production of the relatively large eggs than males in the production of tiny sperm. Therfore, offspring are "worth more" for the female than for the male. Females almost never abandon their brood.

Behavior Problems in the Aquarium

In the aquarium, fish pursue the same propagation strategies as in the wild. But since conditions in the aquarium differ from those in nature, fish that exhibit perfectly normal behavior often reduce their number of offspring and cause frustration for the aquarium keeper. The behavior of aquarium fish should not be judged by the standards of human morality but should be understood from the perspective of biological survival.

Aggressiveness Toward Females
Male cichlid and labyrinth fish are often very aggressive toward females. In the aquarium males may kill females prior to spawning, and some may even kill the female after spawning. This happens because the female cannot escape from the territory of the male, as she naturally would in the wild. To us it is incomprehensible that the male would kill a potential mating partner, since this seems to lessen his reproductive success. But nature "thinks" otherwise. Here are a few reasons for this aggressiveness:

Males of East African mouthbreeders are always ready to spawn; in the wild are sought by the females only for this purpose. After spawning the female takes the eggs into her mouth and departs. If a male were to tolerate a female in his territory that is not ready to spawn, it would decrease his chances of propagation. The females of these species also display aggressive behavior toward each other.

Once a female has established herself somewhere, she drives away all the other females. This further decreases the opportunity for the male to mate with a female that is ready to spawn.

Male labyrinth fish that build foam nests are also aggressive toward females, even though they are not always ready to spawn (since they care for the brood in the nest). The shorter the interval between broods, the more offspring the male can produce. Therefore it would be senseless for him to tolerate near the nest a female that is not ready to spawn. In the meantime, he could mate with a ready female and raise another brood.

What you should know about breeding. In breeding labyrinth fish, cichlids, and other aggressive species provide adequate hiding places into which the females can retreat. Be alert and remove any females that are being persecuted.

Aggressiveness Toward Mates and Young in Brood-Tending Fish
Pair-forming cichlids normally share in the defense of territory and caring for the brood. However, when the fish are perturbed, the pairs may break up. The partners then become aggressive toward each other, eat the eggs or the young, and sometimes often the male may kill the female.

Eggs and the young will normally be eaten if the environmental conditions are such that the young have no chance of survival. The parents lessen their reproductive success if they invest time and energy in a senseless attempt at rearing a brood. It is advantageous for the survival of their genes to eat the doomed brood and use it as a rich source of protein. They can then seek out an area with better environmental conditions and rear a new brood with better chances of survival.

What you should know about breeding.
• Keep cichlids in adequately sized aquariums (see pages 111 to 125) with many hiding places. Don't change anything in the tank equipment. Avoid noise and tank vibrations; also avoid a major cleanup of the aquarium or the room when the cichlids begin to rear their brood.
• Put a few surface fish of other species in the tank. These will be regarded by the cichlids as a

threat to their brood and will bind the pair more closely, so that they will be less likely to split up.
• If brood-tending fish in the aquarium eat their young, it is an indication that something may be wrong with the maintenance conditions. Examine the general maintenance conditions and avoid all outside disturbances.

Free-spawning Fish that Eat Their Eggs
In the aquarium, characins, carp, tiger fish, and armored catfish often eat their eggs after spawning. When these fish spawn in their natural habitat, they travel hundreds of yards and distribute their eggs among plants or on the water floor. Thus they are far removed from their eggs. If they find any eggs, most likely they are not their own. Fish eggs are rich in protein and thus are a good food source. Fish that consume the eggs of their competitors relieve their own young of some of the competition for food, spawning places, and other essentials of life.
Aquarium hobbyists often try to wean their fish away from eating eggs by feeding them during spawning. The fish eat the food given them—but they also eat the eggs.
What you should know about breeding. Watch over the fish as much as possible during spawning. Protect the spawn by any available means (see Spawn Grates, page 21 and Spawning Plants, page 22).

Development from Egg to Fry

With most fish, fertilization takes place outside the body. Egg and sperm cells are released into the water, and the sperm cells swim toward to the eggs. Every egg cell can be fertilized by only one sperm cell, because the micropyle (the opening in the cell membrane that allows a sperm cell to enter) closes immediately after a sperm has reached the interior of the egg. The cell begins to divide—first into two daughter cells, then into four, eight, 16, 32, and so on. This does not affect the entire cell but only the yolk-poor area on the so-called animal pole of the cell. The fertilized egg develops gradually as the cells continue to divide and differentiate into organs and body parts. Development of the embryos proceed at different rates in different species of aquarium fish. Lesser variations in the rate of development may also occur within embryos of a given species. See the illustration on page 53 for a typical calendar of events in the development of the eggs of a mouthbreeder, from several days after fertilization to hatching.

Reproductive Biology and Fish Behavior

Egg Development in a Mouthbreeder
Eggs of mouthbreeders develop much more slowly than those of other species.

1. Seven days after fertilization. The first structures are formed at the animal pole of the egg cell. The eyes are already recognizable.

2. After 14 days. The shape of the larvae can already be seen. The larvae are closely bound to the yolk sac, and the eyes are now fully formed.

3. After 18 days. The larvae have made considerable progress in freeing themselves from the yolk sac. The fins are beginning to take shape.

4. After 21 days. The fins are now clearly recognizable. The larva form has been replaced by fully developed fry.

5. After 28 days the fry have almost consumed their yolk sac.

6. After 35 days the young emerge from the mother's mouth and can now eat independently.

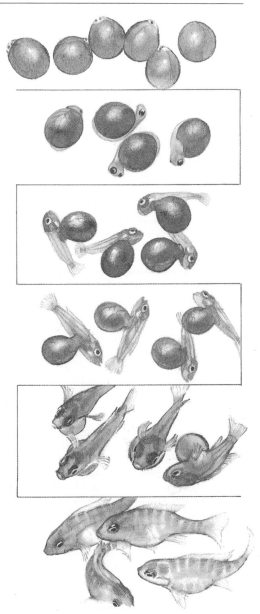

Practical Guidelines for Fish Breeding

Choosing the Right Fish

Fish that are to produce many healthy offspring should be of the right age and should not show signs of disease.

Important. If you want to breed several generations of fish, you should buy several pairs of males and females. This will help you to avoid inbreeding.

Age

With many fish the best breeding results are obtained right after sexual maturity, when the animals have reached full coloration but are not yet fully grown. The small, short-lived species from the flood areas of tropical rivers (many characins and barbs) are at the peak of their productivity during the first or second year of life. In the wild most of them die after the first reproductive period following the rainy season, when the water drains from the flooded areas. Long-lived fish, on the other hand (such as like large cichlids and catfish), can produce several generations of strong off-spring.

When does sexual maturity occur in fish? The sexual maturity of fry just like their general development, depends on the water temperature, water quality, and the food supply. Cool water, a high nitrate content, and an inadequate diet retard sexual maturity.

Under normal conditions most fish species reach sexual maturity between the fifth and eighth months. Larger cichlids become sexually mature only after nine to 12 months; discus fish require about 18 months.

Live-bearing toothed carp can attain sexual maturity after only six to eight weeks. Observe the fry closely and separate the sexes as soon as the gonopodium (sexual organ) of the young males begins to form.

Egg-laying toothed carp and other *Nothobranchius* and *Cynolebias* species are the fastest to mature. They are ready to reproduce two to five weeks after emerging from the eggs.

Health

Do not breed sick or deformed fish. Also avoid pairing fish that, even under the best rearing conditions, produce crippled young or lay eggs that do not develop. These should be excluded from further attempts at breeding.

How to recognize healthy fish.

• Healthy fish possess the body shape typical of their species.

• They have no deformities (for example, curvature of the spine, shortened or deformed jaw, deformed gill covering).

• The fins should not appear frayed or fused.

• White, coarse spots; a cottonlike, white coating; or a dull skin are clear indications of disease.

• Healthy fish have strong colors.

• They swim around animatedly, without jerky movements.

• They show the typical behavior of their species (for example, swimming in the lower, middle or upper region of the tank; schools of fish swim in groups, not singly).

Larvophile mouthbreeders during spawning activity.

Cichlids of the *Geophagus surinamensis* group, which includes other closely related ovophile mouthbreeders. Above: The pair are polishing the spawning bed. This removes organic pollutants, and the eggs cling better. Below: Egg laying and fertilization often take place intermittently. After the female lays the eggs, the parents clean and fan the spawn. When the larvae emerge they are taken into the parents' mouths. Even after swimming independently for a while, they return to the protective mouths of the parents.

Practical Guidelines for Fish Breeding

Maintenance of Breeding Fish until Spawning

If you maintain your fish in clean water and in accordance with the requirements of the species, you have already taken the first step toward successful breeding. Aquarium hobbyists normally keep their animals in completely equipped community aquariums or species tanks.

The tank equipment must be attuned to the needs of the fish. Determine in detail the needs of the fish species that you would like to breed. The fish will be motivated to reproduce in the aquarium only when all the factors are favorable.

Here are a few general suggestions:

• Fish that live in schools need a large swimming area in the middle and foreground of the aquarium. The sides and background should be planted, so that individual fish can hide among the plants.

• Catfish and loaches should have dugouts and caves.

• Cichlids, in addition to caves, need stone towers (stones placed one on top of the other) or vertical stone disks (reinforced by smaller stones at the bottom) as territorial boundaries.

• Fish from dark tropical forest waters need floating plants that dim the light.

Clean, oxygen-rich water can be maintained by regularly cleaning your filters (so that they don't get clogged up) and changing the aquarium water.

Plants in the aquarium serve not only as decorations or hiding places for the fish, but also as a means of water purification. The plants absorb nitrogen compounds that are produced by fish droppings and dead bacteria. Choose plants known for their water-purifying characteristics. The best of these are the waterweed species (*Egeria, Elodea*), all *Hygrophila* species, all floating plants (especially the water hyacinth *Eichhornia crassipes*), and duckweed (*Lemma*).

A community tank requires special caution.

• Don't keep small fish together with large fish who will chase them.

• Do not combine placid fish, which like to be motionless among plants, with fish that like a strong current.

Feeding with live food (see Types of Food and Feeding page 41) is essential for motivating fish to spawn in the aquarium.

Transferring for breeding. Here are two general suggestions. You will find precise instructions later in the book (see page 70 to 132).

• Fish that live in schools and do not care for their young (such as characins and barbs) are taken out of the maintenance tank mostly in pairs or in small groups and put in spawning tanks which hold the breeding water. After spawning they are returned to the maintenance tank.

• Territorial fish (such as cichlids and labyrinth fish) stay in their aquarium right up to spawning. Transferring them to a new environment cari upset territorial fish so much that they don't spawn at all, or that they eat their eggs or young. The stress of transferring and the unfamiliar atmosphere sometimes evokes agression in the fish, which can end with the death of the weaker partner.

Care of the Young

Rearing the young of brood-tending fish requires less exertion by the aquarium hobbyist than in the case of species that do not care for their young.

When danger threatens and often at night "dirt eating" cichlids (*Geophagus steindachneri*) take even older fry into their mouths. One can see that the fry themselves seek out the mother's mouth and are not merely collected.

Barbs at spawning. The male (front) lays his tail fin over the female.

Fish that Care for Their Young

With these species the parents care for the eggs and rear their young. The amateur breeder, as a rule, need only be concerned about proper food for the fry.

When brood tending fish abandon their brood or devour it. This occurs when the fish are upset by unfavorable environmental conditions (see page 52). In such a case you can do the following:
• Transfer the spawn into a rearing tank, and leave the parents in the breeding tank. The water in the rearing tank should be of the same quality as that in the breeding tank.
• If the eggs were deposited on wood, a stone, or in a cave (as happens most often), take them out together with the material on which they are found and put them in the rearing tank in the same position as before.
• If the eggs adhere to plant leaves, cut the leaves and transfer them to the rearing tank together with the eggs.
• Always lift the eggs together with the material to which they are attached. Transfer them to a container filled with breeding water. In this way they are less likely to be harmed and be susceptible to bacteria and fungi.
• Add a disinfectant to the water in the rearing tank if necessary.
• The eggs of mouth-breeding cichlids (mouth-breeding cichlids often spit out their eggs if they are transferred shortly after spawning) cannot be treated as described above. In nature they are constantly moved and turned in the mouth of the brood-tending fish, and they require such move-ment. If they just lie in the rearing tank, they will die. Even if air is circulated around the eggs in the rearing tank, the results will not be good. Rearing these fry without the brood-tending parents often produces poor brood-tending aquarial stock. All this expense should be incurred only if you want to maintain a rare fish species.

Fish that Do Not Care for Their Young

With these species you will have to concern yourself with the rearing of the young. Two methods are recommended; depending on the species:
• With fish that deposit all their eggs at once, take the parents out of the breeding tank after spawning, and let eggs develop in the tank.
• With fish that deposit small numbers of eggs from time to time, place the eggs in a rearing tank, and leave the parents in the breeding tank.
Eggs that sink to the ground are sucked up with a tube. If the eggs cling to plants or to other objects, separate the eggs from the objects (always use a clean container with breeding water). Insensitive eggs (such as those of many egg-laying toothed carp) are carefully gathered up from the spawning bed. Eggs that float on the water surface can be scooped up with a spoon.

Feeding the Young

When the fish larvae emerge from the eggs, they still have their yolk sac, which they devour—

depending on the species—during the first hours or days after emergence. They then begin to swim and to hunt for food. You must now provide for them the proper food, tailored to their size. Without the right live food the young will not survive.

Ground rules. The live food should be about as big as the eye of the fry.

• Very small fry (like those of many labyrinth fish) are nourished during the first few days with infusorians (microorganisms, protozoa).

• Somewhat bigger fry are nourished with creatures such as rotifers, which lack skeletons.

• Still bigger, less delicate fry (such as those of live-bearing toothed carp) can be brought up on finely ground dry food or, if necessary, hard-boiled crushed egg yolk.

Several other food preparations for smaller and bigger fry can be obtained in tropical fish stores. Herviborous fish receive algae, crushed plant parts, or food with an agar base.

Recipe for Agar Paste

For this paste agar powder is combined with different food mixtures.

Food mixture 1: In a mortar grind up 1 teaspoon each of the following ingredients: 1 teaspoon each dry food, dried *Daphnia*, shrimp chips, egg powder (all obtainable in a pet shop), carrot and algae meal (obtainable at a health food store), and bone meal (found in a garden supply shop). Store in a tightly sealed jar in the refrigerator until further processing.

Food mixture 2: In a mixer blend the following ingredients: about $1^1/_4$ pound (125 g) each of fresh fish meat (two kinds) and shrimp. Freeze the mixture in ice cube trays.

Dissolve about 2 cubic inches (5 cm³) of agar powder in about $^1/_{10}$ quart (100 ml) of boiling water. Cool to about 120°F (50°C).

Preparation of the paste: Blend together the hot agar solution (at about 120°F), 1 teaspoon of food mixture 1, 1 thawed cube of food mixture 2, 1 pinch of celery powder, a few drops of multivitamin preparation, and let it cool. A thick gel will form, which you can cut into cubes and preserve in the refrigerator. Prepare the cubes for food by

sifting them through a sieve. The mixture doesn't cloud the water.

Cultivation of Live Food for Fry

Fry today are fed mostly with homegrown live food, since it is becoming ever harder to find clean water in which to catch the small organisms. Homegrown live food transmits no diseases and contains no environmental pollutants.

Paramecia

These one-celled microorganisms (protozoa) develop in water contamining organic substances.

How paramecia are bred. Fill tall jelly jars with stagnant tap water and insert a few pieces of turnip (*Brassica napus*). Other turnip species will not do. "Inject" this culture with paramecia, (for example, water from oxygen-deficient puddles). When the turnip fragments start to decompose, bacteria develop and use up the oxygen in the water. The paramecia feed on these bacteria. Since nearly all other organisms except the bacteria and paramecia perish from lack of oxygen, paramecia are obtained in a pure culture in the upper part of the jar, which still contains some oxygen. Occasionally, instead of a turnip, add a teaspoonful of millk; the cultures will then not stick as much.

Paramecia cultures in granular form are available in pet shops. The prescribed amount is added to the water, and the paramecia develop after several days. Such cultures often contain other microorganisms that can harm sensitive fry. For very small and delicate fry paramecia from proper turnip cultures are recommended.

How to prepare paramecia as food. Remove the upper layer of water in the breeding jar and filter it through a sieve of fine silk gauze. For sturdier fry (for example, those of the speckled armored catfish), you can transfer the paramecia directly into the tank water. Delicate fry, however, cannot tolerate the bacteria in the water of the breeding jar. For them you must purify the paramecia before using them as food.

How to purify paramecia. Fill a tall test tube, Erlenmeyer flask, or a glass tube about 20 inches (50 cm) long and about $1^1/_5$ inches (3 cm) in diameter about two-thirds full with water from the upper layer of a paramecium culture. On the water surface place a piece of cotton wadding or a very fine cork and over it pour stagnant, chlorine-free tap water to a height of about 4 inches (10 cm). Since the oxygen in the water decreases, the paramecia crawl through the cork into the clean water above; from there they can be sucked up with a pipette and fed to the fry. The paramecium trap, available in pet shops, operates on the same principle. You simply attach it to the breeding jar.

Euglena *(Euglena viridis)*

Euglena are one-celled organisms that behave like plants during the day (they are green; absorb light, water, and CO_2; and emit oxygen) and like animals at night (they lose their green color and feed on bacteria and other small organisms). In the dark, euglena colonies develop an unpleasant odor, because bacteria are formed by putrefaction

Brood-tending characins (Lebiasinidae) at spawning. The male (front) tends the brood. Brood tending is rare in characins.

processes. Illuminated euglena cultures, on th other hand, do not have an unpleasant odor.
How euglena are bred. Fill large jelly jars wit stagnant water, place on a bright but not sunn window, and add a euglena starter culture. Th creatures are obtained from shaded pools or sr green-colored ponds. (Examine with a magnif glass or a microscope to determine whether th green color is due to green algae.) Feed the eu with real beef broth every few days. When the water turns emerald green, the euglena can be prepared for food. Store excess euglena in the and stop feeding them. When they are exposed bright light, they will multiply again.
How euglena are prepared as food. Euglena do need to be cleaned. They are well suited for ver small or small-mouthed fry, especially for speci sensitive to bacteria.

Brine Shrimp *(Artemia salina)*

Brine shrimp are found in salt lakes and on man ocean coasts. Artemia eggs should never becom damp. If kept in airtight jars, they maintain their vitality for years. Shrimp brine can replace the food you have collected if they are not fed exclusively over a long period of time. This type feeding can cause illness in freshwater fish, because they can't tolerate the salty food for long Many adult fish (for example, cichlids) enjoy eating brine shrimp.
How to breed brine shrimp. For small users brine shrimp breeding starters are available in pet shops For many breeders these bottles are too small; the use large jars or small aquariums. These jars are filled to half their volume with salt water, prepare by adding about $3/4$ ounce (20g) sea salt per quart (liter) of water (do not use cooking salt or cooking salt containing iodine). The water is aerated with airstones. One to two teaspoons of brine shrimp (available at pet shops) are added the breeding jar, depending on the amount of water, and shaken. Depending on the temperature of the water the brine shrimp emerge after one to two days. Under bright light you can see the tiny whittish to red creatures swimming after they emerge.

Practical Guidelines for Fish Breeding

How to prepare brine shrimp as food. About ten minutes before feeding, take the airstone out of the breeding jar. The eggs (from which no brine shrimp have yet emerged), settle to the ground. The empty eggshells float on the water surface. Now with the help of a tube let the breeding water run through a fine-meshed sieve of silk gauze or a brine shrimp sieve (both available in pet shops.) The brine shrimp can be used as food without additional cleaning. They contain no freshwater infusorians that can attack the brood. Fill the breeding jar again and add fresh eggs.

My suggestion: Since the development of the eggs lasts about two days, it is recommended that you start three different breeding jars from time to time. The second is filled a day after the first, and the third is filled a day after the second. You can reduce the time of egg development to about 30 hours if you heat the water to about 82°F (28°C). Thus you can have a jar with freshly hatched brine shrimp every day.

Warning: Salty breeding water can ruin furniture. Commercial breeding equipment is leak proof.

Eel Worms (*Anguillla siusia*)
These small (approximately 2 mm long), threadlike worms are raised in breeding boxes in a manner similar to white worms (see page 42).
How eel worms are bred. The breeding containers must not smell of plastic, otherwise the organisms will not be eaten by the fry. The eel worms can be fed a viscous mash of oat flakes, milk and cereal flakes to which a vitamin preparation can be added. The most favorable propagating temperature is 77°F (25°C).
Preparing eel worms as food. The creatures crawl to the side walls of the breeding container and can be taken up with a razor blade or with the forefinger and put into the aquarium. Very delicate, sensitive fry do not tolerate the bacteria carried over from the food mash. The eel worms are eaten with relish by young catfish, cichlids, and barbs, which prefer to take their food on the ground.

Japanese Water Fleas
Starter cultures for this small water flea, which is relatively resistant to high temperature and lack of oxygen, are often offered in the classified section of aquarists' magazines. The offspring of this species can be used as a valuable food for bigger fry. These fleas are raised like other water fleas (see page 43) but at higher temperatures (therefore, in a regular room).

Pond Food

If you are fortunate enough to find clean ponds or puddles in your neighborhood, do not deprive yourself of the pleasure of collecting food.

Laetacaria curviceps cichlids during brood tending. These open breeders splash water to their spawn and clean the eggs. The male and female alternate every few minutes.

Rotifers (Rotatoria) are a very important rearing food that can be given to most fry after they become free swimming. Rotifers are caught in the summer in warm, somewhat shaded ponds and puddles. Frozen rotifers from pet shops are ready as food when thawed.

Practical Guidelines for Fish Breeding

Cyclops larvae are also eaten with relish by fry. The water flea *Cyclops* is a prey snatcher that captures and devours small water organisms. *Cyclops larvae* therefore should be prepared as food in small amounts, since in the higher temperatures of the tropical aquarium they develop quickly into adults that can capture tiny fry. *Cyclops* develop in the colder season, even under ice. In the summer they are found only in cool, shaded pools.

Diaptomus larvae feed on microorganisms and algae, which they filter out of the water. In contrast to *Cyclops*, *Diaptomus* larvae do not hop but glide evenly through the water. They hop only when they are frightened. Adult *Diaptomus* fleas have much longer antennae (feelers) than *Cyclops*. Since both kinds can be well differentiated from each other, it is preferable to offer your fish the safe *Diaptomus* larvae. Like *Cyclops*, they are also found under ice in the cold season; in summer you can find them in cool, shaded ponds.

Daphnia, the typical water fleas, are not suitable food in the first days after the fry become free swimming. They are too big. But for grown fry they are among the most important food sources. *Daphnia* are found in great numbers in shallow, warm water. You can settle them in your garden pond and feed them now and then with yeast, fish food, sap, or horse manure.

Bosmina are small crustaceans, but they have such a hard shell that they are only eaten by robust fry. In the warm season they can be found on shallow sea coasts, where they are driven by wind and currents.

Equipment for Collecting Pond Food

Pond food can be collected with fishing nets of various mesh widths, portable containers, and sieves.

Nets
Pet shops have ready-made fishing nets with metal clasps that stick together. You can also make your own nets. For this purpose use very fine needles,

gauze and nylon yarn to sew a pouch about 12 inches (30 cm) in diameter and 20 to 27 inches (50 to 70 cm) in length. This net is sewn onto a rust proof metal ring of the corresponding diameter. The metal ring and net are fastened to a stick about 2 yards (2 m) long (broomsticks and sticks for garden equipment are too short). For material for the net you can use nylon or gauze. The best suited is silk gauze, which can be obtained in pet shops or in zoological laboratory supply stores.

• *Daphnia*, gnat larvae, and larvae of large insects can be captured with coarser nets.
• Silk gauze with a mesh width of 130/1000 mm and 106/1000 mm is most often used to capture small organisms, such as rotifers.
• Silk gauze with a mesh width of 85/1000 mm is suited for the very smallest organisms. Drag the net through the water using a float, and empty the catch into a portable container.

Red neons spawn in shoals. Like many school fish, neons cannot be placed in pairs for spawning. They need to be in a group for spawning to occur.

Practical Guidelines for Fish Breeding

Portable Containers

The containers should be as flat and wide as possible. The greater the water surface area, the more oxygen will be absorbed by the water. Hot water absorbs less oxygen than cold water. Therefore, in hot weather collect fewer organisms in each container.

Sieves

In every catch organisms of various sizes remain in the net; only those small enough to crawl through the mesh can escape. These organisms must be sorted according to size by using sieves with standard mesh widths. Pet shops have plastic sieves with standard mesh widths. If you do not have many fish, you can use sieves about 4 inches (10 cm) in diameter. If you keep many fish or raise large broods, you should choose larger ones. Dip a sieve with the proper mesh width for the food at hand into the water of the rearing tank or let it float on the water surface. Then add some of the pond food and shake carefully. Creatures that escape through the mesh get into the rearing tank and are eaten by the fry. All other organisms remain in the sieve and are given to larger fry or to adult fish.

How Much and How Often to Feed

You can let adult fish go without food now and then, but never young fry. You should never put a large amount of live food into the tank, because the organisms die off after a while, decompose, and contaminate the water. Or (like *Cyclops*) they may grow so fast that they attack the fry.

Fry should be fed four to six times a day and should receive as much as they can consume in 15 minutes. Working people, who can feed the fish only in the morning and evening, must either feed them copiously twice a day or rely on the help of their family or neighbors. Automatic feeders for live food have been developed. For example, one can let water from a paramecium culture drip slowly through a thin air hose into the aquarium. The adjustment of the water flow must be carefully controlled. If too little gets into the aquarium, the young will go hungry: if too much is delivered the organisms will die and pollute the water.

Feeding nonchasing fry. Young glass perch (*Chanda ranga*) do not hunt for food, but eat only what floats directly in front of their mouths. One would have to feed them so much that the fry would be "swimming in food," and the water would be contaminated with decomposition products. To remedy the situation, use the following ruse. Darken the tank with paper and leave a hole on one side. Near the hole install a dim bulb that will illuminate only a small section of the tank. The light attracts the live food and the fry, so that the latter can easily eat the prey. All leftover dead food is carefully sucked up during the water change.

Feeding growing fry. As the fry grow older, they should receive even larger and more nourishing live food; they should also get slowly accustomed to food flakes and pellets. Older fry like to eat *Daphnia* and eel worms. White worms (*Enchytraea*) are fattening and should not be fed often to fry—except to fast-growing cyprinodonts (see Egg-laying Toothed Carp, page 95), which reach sexual maturity two to three weeks after emergence from the eggs.

Ready-Made Food

Ready-made food for rearing robust as well as small and delicate species of fry is available in pet shops. You can even get food for young discus cichlids. This is a substitute for the body mucus of the parent fish on which the young fry feed during the first few days. Fry of other species can also be well-nourished with this discus-rearing food. Less delicate fish (such as young catfish, many labyrinth fish, and most cichlids) can be fed ready-made liquid or dry food (such as Mardel's Aquarium Growth Food) during the first two to three days, and then can be switched over to *Artemia* (brine shrimp). This avoids the use of strong-smelling paramecium culture.

Unusual spawning. The red-tailed carp belongs to the killifish. As in the rice fish (see illustration, page 41), the eggs are fertilized while the female still carries them with her. In the red-tailed carp some of the eggs are suspended by long threads.

Diseases of Fish

All fish are vulnerable to disease under certain conditions.
• Fish tuberculosis often results from errors in faulty maintenance (for example, an overcrowded aquarium, inadequate feeding, or a dirty filter).
• Intestinal diseases (such as ascites) can be caused by too cold or spoiled food.
• Infectious diseases such as *Hexamita* and *Columnaris* can befall weakened fish.
• Skin parasites can be introduced by new fish that had not previously been quarantined.
You can get detailed information about diseases in the specialized literature. Your pet dealer will recommend the proper medicine.

Ground rules.
• The best preventive measures are optimal maintenance conditions. Therefore, provide a spacious aquarium with good filtering and food rich in variety.
• Fish that have been beset by parasites or that have just recovered from a serious disease should not be used for breeding.
Some diseases and injuries are of special interest to the breeder. They concern the reproductive organs, eggs, embryos, and fry.

Diseases and Injuries of the Reproductive Organs
Fatty degeneration. Males and females with fatty degeneration are severely limited in their reproductive capacity. Very fat females often cannot discharge their spawn. Fatty testicles produce fewer sperm.
Hardening, clumping, and partial drying of the spawn can also be caused by infections (such as tuberculosis or *Ichthyosporidium*) or by parasites (for example, nematodes of the genera *Capillaria* and *Philometra*).
Spawn suppression (when females can no longer lay their spawn) can be caused by a deficiency of trace elements or by unfavorable environmental conditions (for example, a too high temperature).
Ovarian cysts or tumors often develop when females cannot lay their spawn (see above).
Preventive measures: include optimal maintenance conditions and precaution against infectious diseases and parasites. Avoid feeding with live food.

Diseases and Injuries of Eggs, Embryos, Larvae, and Fry
Spawn fungus is caused by the water fungus *Saprolegnia*, which can also attack weak or very sick adult fish. The fungi attacks mostly unfertilized eggs and those that are dead or have been damaged by lack of oxygen. If allowed to spread unchecked, the fungus can destroy the entire spawn.
Preventive measures: After spawning filter out the sperm (see page 16) in order to deprive the fungi of their food source. Disinfect the water (see page 67). Collect all unfertilized and dead eggs before the fungus develops.

Practical Guidelines for Fish Breeding

Damage to eggs and embryos from lack of oxygen is often irreversible. If the oxygen content of the water is too low, cell division in the eggs slows down or stops entirely. If the oxygen deprivation is not prolonged, cell division may resume (or speed up), but is usually defective, and the embryos are so severely damaged that they die in the egg. The few that do emerge usually have very serious deformities.

Preventive measures: Clean the water. Use powerful filters. Do not allow bacteria to develop; they use up oxygen (see page 67).

Damage to eggs due to health disturbances in the parents. Lack of vitamins and trace elements or infectious diseases can damage the eggs even in the mother's body so that they no longer have a chance for development. The yolk curdles, the eggs become soft and spotted, and they crumble. Deformities can be caused not only by a lack of oxygen but also by vitamin deficiency. Skeletal deformities can be caused by fish tuberculosis and *Ichthyosporidium* in the parents.

Brood-tending angelfish. A parent removes dead eggs (those that have become white).

Preventive measures: Use healthy fish for breeding.

Attacks on the eggs and fry by larger aquatic animals.

• Planaria are small flatworms (*Plathelminthes*) scarcely an inch (2 cm) long that attack the spawn in normally equipped species aquariums (especially at night). They are introduced with live pond food. Brood-tending fish eat the worms, but they cannot always save the spawn if the infestation is severe. Planaria also interfere with breeding because they use up oxygen.

Remedy: Remove the fish from the tank, and raise the water temperature to 90–95°F (32–35°C). If the planaria are still alive, empty the aquarium and disinfect the tank and all equipment (see page 67).

• Hydra, the water polyp, is also introduced with live pond food. The creatures attach themselves to plants, glass panes, and decorative objects and catch small fry that wander into their area.

Remedy: Use the same measures as with planaria (see above).

• *Costia*, *Chilodonella* (unicellular skin parsites), and *Oodinium* (the microorganism that causes "velvet disease") occasionally attack fry.

Remedy: These parasites can be controlled with commercial fish medicines available in pet shops. Skin parasites can also be destroyed with trypaflavine. It should be given at a concentration of 1:100,000 (1g to 100 liters) in breeding tanks.

My recommendation: Get yourself a strong magnifying glass and a small microscope so that you can follow the development of the eggs, the condition of the larvae, and the fry. Even the cultivation of live food is more easily controlled with a magnifying glass. A magnifying glass (and, in many cases, a microscope) is indispensable for the diagnosis of diseases.

Breeding Fish that Require a Rainy Season

For most tropical fish the beginning of the rainy season is the trigger for spawning. In the violent tropical storms huge amounts of rain fall over a short period of time, and the rivers rise rapidly. The rainwater greatly dilutes the river water. The water thus becomes softer and its nitrogen content decreases. The food supply also changes. In the dry season many fish live on very meager food and even on fallen tree fruit. Now they have an abundant supply of insect larvae and other invertebrate animals.

Creating a Rainy Season in the Aquarium

When you take fish out of the community aquarium and put them in a breeding tank, you are recreating the conditions of a tropical storm. The fish are transferred from the semihard, somewhat dirty water of the community tank into very soft, clean water, which nearly corresponds to rainwater. In addition, they are given abundant live food (black gnat larvae for the smaller fish and *Mysis* for the bigger fish). With the commonly bred species the change of water and food is sufficient to motivate them to spawn. In some species it was shown that the sex organs mature during the water changes at the beginning of the rainy season. Knifefish of the genus *Eigenmannia* (in particular the green knifefish (*E. virescens*) were bred as follows. For about six weeks the rainy season was imitated by slowly adding fully desalted water (about 5% of the tank volume) each day to a tank initially half full. In this way the salt content and pH value of the breeding water decreased, while the water level rose. In addition, a rain shower was simulated for several hours a day by spraying the filter water onto the water surface. When the tank was full, half of it was emptied, and the procedure was begun again. After the first spawning, additional simulation is not necessary but it is desirable sporadically as long as the desired water quality is maintained.

This method will surely achieve importance among aquarists in the future, especially for the breeding of many fish regarded as "unbreedable" (for example, certain loaches and catfish).

Almost classic is the breeding of the armored catfish (*Callichthys callichthys* and *Hoplosternum thoracatum*), which live in the flood areas of the South American rivers. During the dry season they await the next rainfall in the slowly drying swamp pools. They can suck in air, absorbing the oxygen through their rectum, and thus survive when the water is almost gone. As soon as it rains, the males build nests which they secure with plant parts and leaves.

In the aquarium armored catfish were stimulated to breed by splashing them with water from a watering can. The next day the males began to build a nest, and the pair spawned. During the last decade these fish have become so well adjusted to the conditions of the aquarium that today they rarely need rainwater. Lowering of the water hardness (conductivity) is sufficient for them to start breeding.

Many fish that have not previously been kept in an aquarium require a greater degree of simulation of the environmental conditions in the native habitat. Certain antenna catfish of the genus *Pimelodus* have been observed to mate when they were illuminated by lightning flashes or flashes from a stroboscope. Even loud rock music (with frequencies similar to those of thunderclaps) is said to have motivated catfish and other tropical fish to mate—but not yet to spawn. One might then try to stage tropical storms similar those used in zoological gardens to induce crocodiles to mate. Treatment with sex hormones, as practiced by commerical animal collectors, is taboo for the aquarium hobbyists.

Simulating a Tropical Storm

Rain. Spray lukewarm water from a watering can into the aquarium. Fully desalted water from the ion exchanger (see page 29) or the reverse osmosis apparatus (see page 31) is more effective than tap water.

Lightning. If possible flash light from above, (not from the side), into the tank. You can use the flash equipment of your camera or install a stroboscope (small stroboscopes are available in toy stores). Even disco lamps produce beautiful flashes.

Thunder. Vibrate a thin aluminum cake pan in front of the microphone of a sound-recording apparatus. Make it rattle loudly. If you don't have thin cake pans, you can also use strong aluminum foil. A cheap cassette recorder is better suited for this task than an expensive machine. The cassette

Practical Guidelines for Fish Breeding

recorder reproduces with less accuracy and thus the sound of the "thunder" becomes more credible. Let this glorious tropical storm run its course for a good half hour or a whole hour. But bear in mind that "tropical storms" after 10 p.m. in the evening can take place only if the sound of the storm does not carry beyond own apartment.

Disinfection and Cleaning of Aquariums

Disinfection of aquariums and breeding water is necessary if you breed delicate fish species. For these fish the water must not only be kept free of nitrogen compounds (see page 34) and phosphates (see page 36), but should contain no bacteria, infusorians, or viruses.

Warning: Do not disinfect species tanks equipped for brood-tending fish. That would kill the plants and bacteria and would upset the equilibrium of the entire system. Brood-tending fish remove unfertilized and dead eggs themselves and fan fresh water to the spawn. Frequently they also clean the eggs, so that bacteria and fungi have no chance to harm them.

Disinfection of Spawning Tanks

For very delicate fish species and for those that do not care for their young, you should disinfect the spawning and rearing tanks prior to installation.
Disinfectant solutions.

• A weak potassium permanganate solution. Add enough reagent so that the solution is rose colored (it need not be dosed exactly).

• A saturated cooking salt solution. Add enough cooking salt (sodium chloride) into boiling water so that no more will dissolve, then let the solution cool.

• A strong, yellow trypaflavine solution.
Do the following:

• Thoroughly wash tanks, heaters, and spawning grates with one of these solutions.

• Rinse down with cool boiled water.

• Plants for fish sensitive to infusorians are disinfected for five minutes in an alum bath (a heaping teaspoon of alum to 1 quart of water) and then rinsed well.

Additional Measures for Maintaining Cleanliness

Once the fish have been placed in the spawning tank, disinfectants can no longer be used. They would harm the fish and kill their eggs and sperm. Here are some important measures you can take to keep the water clean so that the fish, eggs, and fry remain healthy.

Feed as little as possible. This is necessary to minimize the content of bacteria, infusorians, and nitrites.

Fish that spawn within a few hours or in the first three days after being put in the spawning tank can be allowed to fast or be given a small amount of washed white worms. Many breeders do not feed their fish for several hours before they are placed in the spawning tank, so that the fish will not deposit droppings in the clean water.

Species that spawn continuously over a long period of time cannot be allowed to fast. For these fish you will need a strong filter (see page 15) and constant monitoring of the water quality.

Remove unfertilized eggs and sperm. Unfertilized eggs, surplus sperm, and seminal fluid decompose in the water and provide a fertile food source for bacteria, infusorians, and fungi. These organisms attack healthy eggs and embryos and can destroy the spawn partially or completely. They can also harm the embryos by depriving them of oxygen.

• Brood-tending fish remove unfertilized and dead eggs themselves.

• In peat-filtered water the spawn is not greatly endangered. Peat contains anti-bacterial and anti-fungal agents and the tannic acids strengthen the eggshells.

• With fish that do not care for their young, after spawning filter the water for several hours over activated charcoal or a diatomite filter.

• Remove unfertilized and dead eggs with tweezers. They are opaquely white, while fertilized eggs remain clear.

• Dead eggs with a white coating are infected with fungus and must be destroyed immediately.

Sterilize the water with chemicals. This measure is especially necessary when fish eggs need a longer time to develop, or if (after spawning) the water is not filtered over activated charcoal.

Practical Guidelines for Fish Breeding

Striped Indian cichlid with fry. The fry always travel in schools looking for food, while the parents follow them and look after them.

• Trypaflavine colors the water a fluorescent yellowish green. It is a very strong disinfectant. To prepare a 0.1 percent solution, disssolve 1g trypaflavine in a quart (liter) of distilled water. Add 16.5 ml of this solution for every $2^1/2$ gallons (10 liters) of aquarium water.

Methylene blue and trypaflavin are safe for the fish. Methylene blue is convenient to use because you cannot make any mistakes in the dosage. Trypaflavine has been proven to be effective for the preservation of the eggs of egg-laying toothed carp, while methylene blue is the preferred agent for rearing cichlids and armored catfish. As soon as the young have emerged, the disinfectants are filtered out with activated charcoal.

Caution: Methylene blue and trypaflavine are dyes. Stains on clothing are difficult if not impossible to remove.

Water can also be made relatively germfree with ozone or UV light (see page 40). Familiarize yourself thoroughly with both methods. Ozone harms plants, and UV light should under never be allowed to shine directly on the fish or their brood.

It is very important that you add these chemicals to the water only after the fish have spawned. If you do it beforehand, the delicate sperm will be killed immediately, and the eggs will remain unfertilized.

• Methylene blue is used most frequently. To prepare a 3 percent solution, dissolve about $^1/_{10}$ ounce (3g) methylene blue in about $^1/_5$ pint (97 ml) of water. Pour as much of this solution into the aquarium as will still permit you to recognize the eggs.

• You can also buy ready-made solutions in the pharmacy. Make certain, however, that the methylene blue is dissolved in water. There are also alcoholic solutions, which should not be used in the aquarium.

• Pet shops offer fish medicine that contain the methylene blue. In emergencies you also use this as a disinfectant.

Practical Guidelines for Fish Breeding

A Breeding Plan for Problem Fish—13 Suggestions Based on Experience

Here are some methods that have been proven useful with some fish species. With others you must discover your own through observation.

1. Keep the fish in spacious species aquariums and nourish them optimally (see the chapter on feeding, page 41).

2. Find out from which area and which biotope your fish originate, and equip your aquarium so that they find their hiding places, spawning beds, and all other material that they will need to build their nests.

3. Learn when the rainy season begins in your fishes' habitat. Information about the amount of precipitation and wind current can be found in atlases or almanacs.

4. Ascertain whether the length of day in your fishes' habitat changes with the seasons. At the equator the days and nights are always 12 hours long. With increasing distances from the equator, the days get longer in the summer and shorter in the winter. Regulate the length of the "day" to correspond to the needs of your fish.

5. Prepare your fish to begin breeding at about the same time as they would in their native habitat. Many fish continue their inborn cycles even in the aquarium.

6. Several weeks before the expected breeding period begins, start feeding your fish—but not too abundantly—with nourishing live food (either fresh or frozen).

7. When you think that the females are about to spawn, clean the filter and raise the water temperature about by 2 to 5°F (1 to 3°C). You must clean the filter before the great "downpour" so that the expensive filter bacteria have time to multiply.

8. Drain off water several days to a week after cleaning the filter, drain off about one-half to three quarters of the tank water. Of course, the fish must still be covered.

9. Set up a "storm" using a flash apparatus and noises. Then fill up the tank again by pouring water from above into the tank (with the watering can).

10. Whenever possible use fully desalted water from an ion exchanger (see page 29) or the reverse osmosis equipment (see page 31). This water should be salinized according to the needs of the fish. (2 to 6 dH for fish from tropical rain forest waters).

11. If your aquarium is so small that the "storm" is over when you have emptied three watering cans, remove some water into the can and pour it in again. You must check the pH value and water hardness while the tank is filling up.

12. In some cases you may need to repeat your "storm" several times. During the rainy season in the tropics storms occur almost daily. It is sufficient, however, if you change about one-quarter of the water, or let some tank water run off and spray it back into the aquarium.

13. If despite all this your fish do not reproduce, don't give up. Try to find out sill more about their habits, and you may discover their spawning "trigger."

Breeding Instructions for Aquarium Fish

In this chapter you will be given precise instructions for breeding the most popular aquarium fish. Fish with similar breeding conditions are listed under a common heading. The names of individual species can be obtained from the tables and lists that accompany the text (for example, characins barbels).

There are also fish groups and species for which no common heading can be given, because their requirements are so varied. For these, individual descriptions are provided for each fish (for example, armored catfish).

Whether the breeding information deals with a fish group or with an individual fish, each unit has the same basic structure, so that you can easily make comparisons between individual fish species. The unit structure is composed of the following elements:

Origin and habitat. Here you will find essential information about the habits of the fish that will help you in the proper equipping of the mainte-nance and breeding tanks.

Sexual differences. This information will help you in the purchase and choice of breeding fish.

Maintenance tanks. Proper maintenance is essential for breeding success. If the basic conditions are not right, the fish will not be inclined to reproduce (the females for instance, will not begin to spawn). In this section you will learn whether different fish species can be combined in one aquarium or are better tended in a species tank, you will be given the minimum size of the maintenance tank, and will be informed about the most important equipment.

Water. Here you will learn about the optimal water conditions in preparing the fish for breeding. Fish that are maintained under unfavorable water conditions often do not breed. It is important to note that the water conditions given here do not always coincide with those in a breeding tank, because many fish need a different water quality as a stimulus to spawning. Therefore, you will find water discussed again in the section "Reproduction and Rearing."

Food. If you feed your fish according to these instructions, you will promote their health and their desire to mate.

Reproduction and rearing. In this section you will be given breeding instructions. The text tells you concretely what to do in specific cases and how individual fish behave. This section is divided into the following subsections:

Breeding tanks. Many fish need special conditions for reproduction. Moreover, the majority do not want to be disturbed during mating and spawning. Therefore, it is recommended that almost all fish be put in a special breeding tank for mating.

Water. Here you will learn about the optimal water conditions necessary for the fish to spawn and for the eggs and larvae to develop.

Reproductive behavior. This information will help amateur breeders to recognize reproductive behavior, which is not always easy even for the advanced breeder.

Spawn. The number of eggs laid is based on observation.

Emergence of the young. You will learn about the development of the young until the free-swimming stage, at which time you must begin to feed them and have a live food breeding setup in operation.

Rearing. You will be told about optimal food for rapid and healthy growth, and will be given helpful rearing suggestions.

Characins and Related Fish
(*Characiformes*)

The classification of characins embraces 10 families of which about 1000 species are indigenous to South and Central America and about 200 to Africa. Characins are school fish, often with bright colors, that are active during the day. The colors serve for recognition of the members of the species and therefore the cohesion of the school. Species with luminous markings on their bodies come from dark tropical forest waters: brightly colored and silvery scale-covered species live in the wild in light, more or less clear water.

Characins kept and bred in the aquarium are predominantly from America, especially the genuine American characins, family *Characidae* (see below) and representatives of the family *Lebiasinidae* (see page 76). The African species are represented by the genuine African characins, family *Alestidae* (see page 79).

American Characins
(*Characidae*)

This family includes delicate and more robust species. The delicate species have very demanding water requirements; it must be soft, acidic, and free of bacteria, infusorians, and fungi. Their spawn is very sensitive to light. Always keep characins in schools of at least 7; schools of 15 to 20 fish are even better.

Origin. South and Central America.

Habitat. Flowing and still waters or in dense plant growth.

Sexual differences. Males are smaller and slimmer than females; the anal fin of many species is bordered with small hooks; the dorsal and anal fins are longer and more extended.

Maintenance tanks. Species or community aquarium. Size: side length of at least 24 inches (60 cm). Installation: dark tank bed for species from tropical rain forests; brighter tank bed for characins from sunny brooks. Thick edge and background foliage in which chased fish can hide, (fine-plumed plants are possible). Floating plants for dimming the light for fish from forest areas.

American Characins

Black tetra (*Gymnocorymbus ternetzi*), 2.2 inches (5.5 cm), Bolivia

* *Hasemania nana*, 1.2 inches (3 cm), Brazil

Buenos Aires tetra (*Hemigrammus caudovittatus*), 4 inches (10 cm), La Plata area

* *Hemigrammus erythrozonus*, 1.6 inches (4 cm), British Guayana (see illustration, page 26)

Head and tail light (*Hemigrammus ocellifer*), 1.8 inches (4.5 cm), Amazon area

* Garnet tetra (*Hemigrammus pulcher*), 1.8 inches (4.5 cm), Amazon area

* Rummy-nose tetra (*Hemigrammus rhodostomus*), 1.8 inches (4.5 cm), Amazon delta

* *Hyphessobrycon bentosi*, 1.6 inches (4 cm), lower Amazon area

* Callistus tetra (*Hyphessobrycon callistus*), 1.6 inches (4 cm), southern Amazon area, Paraguay

Flame tetra (*Hyphessobrycon flammeus*), 1.6 inches (4 cm), Brazil

* *Inpaichthys kerri*, 1.6 inches (4 cm), Brazil

* Black neon tetra (*Hyphessobrycon herbertaxelrodi*), 1.6 inches (4 cm), Brazil

* Black phantom tetra (*Megalamphodus megalopterus*), 1.8 inches (4.5 cm), central Brazil

* Swegles' tetra (*Megalamphodus sweglesi*), 1.6 inches (4 cm), northern South America (see illustration page 32)

* Diamond tetra (*Moenkhausia pittieri*), 2.4 inches (6 cm), Venezuela

Moenkhausia sanctaefilomenae, 2.8 inches (7 cm), central South America

* Emperor tetra (*Nematobrycon palmeri*), 2 inches (5 cm), Colombia

* Cardinal tetra (*Paracheirodon axelrodi*), 2 inches (5 cm), Amazon basin (see illustration page 62)

* Common neon tetra (*Paracheirodon innesi*), 1.6 inches (4 cm), upper Amazon area, eastern Peru

Poptella orbicularis, 4.7 inches (12 cm), northern and middle South America

Pristella maxillaris, 1.8 inches (4.5 cm), northern South America

Penguin fish (*Thayeria boehlkei*), 2.4 inches (6 cm), Brazil, Amazon area, Peru

* Delicate species.

Breeding Instructions for Aquarium Fish

Water. Temperature: 73 to 79°F (23 to 26°C) for most species, 70 to 73°F (21 to 23°C) for neon tetras. Water quality: medium hard, lightly acidic (8 to 12 dH, pH about 6.5), rich in oxygen, with minimal amounts of nitrites and nitrates. It is essential to change the water (partially) on a regular basis. In dirty, oxygen poor water characins become pale and languish. The females can no longer deposit their eggs, which leads to hardening of the spawn. Characins from the tropical forest region require peat filtering or a peat supplement.

Food. Small live food (many water fleas and gnat larvae, especially midge larvae just before spawning; small amounts of *Tubifex*; frequent feeding with white worms leads to fatty degeneration and hardening of the spawn), all dry food; plant flakes and other plant food for Buenos Aires tetras, *Poptella*, and *Pristella*.

Breeding suggestion: It's better to give smaller species (for instance, the neon tetra) small food portions several times a day rather than a single large portion.

Reproduction and Rearing

Most characins and similar fish begin to breed in the fall and winter. This is the time that the reproductive period begins in their native habitat, and they have maintained this cycle although many have been bred in captivity for years.

Most characins spawn in pairs; that is, a male and female leave the school and spawn in plant foliage or in open water. Other school members can be stimulated to spawn by the action of the first pair; they pick up the scent of the eggs and sperm or some other spawning material by which their hormones are stimulated. Once they separate into pairs, they do not exchange partners during spawning.

Exceptions. A few characins spawn in schools (for example, the rummy-nose tetra). The fish deposit eggs and sperm simultaneously and constantly exchange partners. However, they spawn almost as well by separating into pairs.

Selection of breeding partners. The best breeding results are achieved if you start with fish that have just become sexually mature (9 to 12 months old).

Older females often suffer from hardening of the spawn and don't produce viable eggs. When possible the male should be older than the female. With species such as the common neon tetra and the flame tetra, which reach the height of their reproductive ability in their first year of life, the female should be 9 to 11 months old and the male, 12 to 15 months. The larger characin species become sexually productive only in their second year, (the female at $1^1/_2$ to 2 years, the male at 2 to $2^1/_2$ years).

Transfer into the breeding tank. The breeding pair is separated from the school and placed in a spare breeding tank (see table, page 75). If the fish are ready, they spawn the morning after being placed in the breeding tank. Therefore, a feeding is unnecessary. If the fish still have not spawned after three days, take them out and put them back into the maintenance tank, then feed them. Many characins spawn four to six times during one reproductive period, with intervals of one to two weeks in between. During the intervals they are put back into the maintenance tank.

Breeding suggestion: If you have enough room and aquariums, separate the male and female during the intervals between spawning and tend to each in a separate tank. Feed them well.

Breeding tanks. The size depends on the size of the fish (see table, page 75) and on their productivity. Equipment: spawning grate or finely plumed plants (see pages 21–24) on the bottom, secured fast with glass rods; one or more of thick plant clusters in which the female can hide. Avoid bright light. Most salmon can't tolerate light during spawning, and the spawn and larvae are often sensitive to it. Use a filter or ventilation.

Mouth breeding Labyrinth fish

Mating ritual in *Betta macrophthalma*:
Top: Male and female approach each other.
Below left: Close embrace during the actual spawning.
Below right: The male gathers the fertilized eggs into his mouth just before they reach the ground. He tends them in his mouth.

Breeding Instructions for Aquarium Fish

Species for breeding aquariums with a capacity of 4 to 5 ¹/₄ gallons (15 to 20 liters)
Hasemania nana
Hemigrammus erythrozonus
Callistus tetra (*Hyphessobrycon callistus*)
Black neon tetra (*Hyphessobrycon herbertaxelrodi*)
Inpaichthys kerri
Swegles' tetra (*Hyphessobrycon sweglesi*)
Nematobrycon palmeri
Cardinal tetra (*Paracheirodon axelrodi*)
Common neon tetra (*Paracheirodon innesi*)

Species for breeding aquariums with a capacity of 13 to 26 gallons (50 to 100 liters)
Buenos Aires tetra (*Hemigrammus caudovittatus*)
Head and tail light (*Hemigrammus ocellifer*)
Garnet tetra (*Hemigrammus pulcher*)
Rummy-nose tetra (*Hemigrammus rhodostomus*), in pairs
Hyphessobrycon bentosi
Flame tetra (*Hyphessobrycon flammeus*)
Black phantom tetra (*Megalamphodus megalopterus*)
Diamond tetra (*Moenkhausia pittieri*)
Moenkhausia sanctaefilomenae
Pristella maxillaris

Species for breeding in aquariums of over 26 gallons (100 liters) (side length of at least 31 inches [80 cm])
Black tetra (*Gymnocorymbus ternetzi*)
Rummy-nose tetra (*Hemigrammus rhodostomus*), best in a school
Poptella orbicularis
Penguin fish (*Thayeria boehlkei*)

Free spawning Labyrinth fish

The kissing gourami (*Helostoma temmincki*) does not bear its name without a reason. The "kissing" is a component of a strong mating, but also a behavior of rival colleagues. Large females can spawn up to 10,000 floating eggs. The eggs rise to the top and most remain clinging to plants.

Breeding suggestion: The eggs and young of most characins are very sensitive to infusorians, bacteria, and other water pollutants. Therefore, prior to installing disinfect the breeding tank, spawning grates, plants, and other equipment (see page 67). Heat the sand and gravel for the tank bed for a few hours in an oven at 428 to 482°F (220 to 250°C). With delicate species (see table page 71) never immerse into the breeding tank the net that you used to remove the fish from the maintenance aquarium.

Water. Temperature: 73.4 to 78.8°F (23 to 26°C) for most characins, 70 to 71.6°F (21 to 22°C) for common neon tetras—above 75.2°F (24°C) their eggs develop badly, 77 to 82.4°F (25 to 28°C) for black tetras. Hardness under 6 dH for delicate species (see table page 71); up to 5 dH for common neon tetras; about 3 dH for cardinal tetras. Many species can be bred in water over 6 dH when the carbonate level is low. The less fastidious species (see table, page 71) can be bred in water of about 15 dH, though a low carbonate level eases spawning for them. pH: between 6 and 7 (peat filtering). Maintenance after spawning: remove fish from the breeding tank; get rid of excess sperm and seminal fluid with an activated charcoal filter. With robust and very productive species (*Poptella orbicularis*), draw off almost all the water from the breeding tank and replace it with fresh water of the same composition and temperature.

Reproductive behavior. All the characins are free spawners, which deposit their eggs in the open water or among plants and then swim away. Most free spawners behave in a characteristic manner. The partners swim vigorously side by side, and the male prods the female with its mouth. He swims in front of her, flutters his fins, then swims ahead of her among the plants. When the female follows, the fish press closely together, holding each other with the pelvic fins. The male hangs on ceremoniously to the female with the hooks on his anal fins. The pair turns completely or partially on its axis and emits eggs and sperm.

Spawn: The eggs fall between the plants or on the ground, since they are not very adhesive. The size of spawn differs from species to species. Common neon tetras produce up to 250 eggs, more productive species produce about 500, and many can lay over 1000 eggs.

Suggestion. If the eggs are attacked by fungus, add trypaflavine to the breeding water after spawning.

Emergence of the young. After about 24 to 36 hours; after five or six days they swim freely.

Rearing: First food: *Artemia* (brine shrimp) larvae for very small fry (for example, those of the common neon tetra and garnet tetra), cleaned paramecia, euglena, and rotifers. Feed often and in small portions, as this has less effect on water quality. Distribute large broods to several large rearing tanks, so that they grow up quickly and uniformly. Change the water daily.

Breeding suggestion: Many young characins also eat finely grated dry food. Such food, however, promotes the development of infusorians and bacteria, which can be deadly for the fry. Feed them only tiny amounts.

Lebiasinidae

The *Lebiasiniadae* are divided into brood-tending species and those that do not care for their young (free spawners).

Free-spawning *Lebiasinidae*

Origin. South America.
Habitat. Small bodies of water.
Sexual differences. Females fatter and often somewhat paler than the males.
Maintenance tanks. Species tanks; community aquarium for small, very peaceful fish. Males build small territories. Size: side length at least 12 inches (30 cm). Equipment: any type of tank bed, not too light. Thick foliage of fine-leaved species; floating plants for subdued light. Slow filter (no strong current).
Water: Temperature: 71.6 to 77°F (22 to 25°C). Hardness: 8 to 12 dH. pH: about 7.
Food: Small live food, mainly insects and insect larvae (*Drosophila*, black midge larvae): also dry food.

Reproduction and Rearing
Fish often don't spawn when the aquarium hobbyist chooses the partners. If you create the optimal maintenance conditions, the fish will pair and begin to mate in the maintenance tank. Transfer the pair into the breeding tank. After spawning remove the parents (separate the male and female if possible) and feed them profusely for about one week.

Breeding tank. Capacity: $2^1/_2$ to 4 gallons (10 to 15 liters). Equipment: no tank bed, install a spawning grate for voracious egg eaters. In the middle of the tank put a Java moss plant, a *Ceratopteris* plant, or a skein of green spawning web, or lay fine-leaved plants on the floor and weight them down with glass rods; for *Nannobrycon* species use a *Cryptocoryne* or sword plant, also weighted down with glass rods.

Water. Temperature: 73.4 to 77°F (23 to 25°C). Hardness: If possible, under 8 dH. pH: 6.5 to 7.5 (filter with peat).

Reproductive behavior. During mating the male swims so closely over the female that he actually "rides" on her. The fish press their bellies close together and deposit the eggs and sperm among the plants. *Nannobrycon* species spawn on the underside of large plant leaves.

Spawn. 30 to 70 eggs.

Emergence of the young. After about 30 to 40 hours; six days after emergence they become free-swimming and start eating.

Rearing. First food: *Artemia* (brine shrimp) larvae; very small fry of the three-lined pencilfish are given cleaned paramecia and euglena. Warning: in the first days of life the fry are very sensitive to light.

Breeding Instructions for Aquarium Fish

Free-spawning *Lebiasinidae*
Nannobrycon eques, 2 inches (5 cm)
Nannobrycon unifasciatus, 2.4 inches (6 cm)
Beckford's pencil fish (*Nannostomus beckfordi*),
2.6 inches (6.5 cm)
Nannostomus bifaciatus, 1.6 inches (4 cm)
Nannostomus digrammus, 1.6 inches (4 cm)
(very fastidious)
Nannostomus espei, 1.4 inches (3.5 cm)
One-lined pencilfish (*Nannostomus marginatus*),
1.4 inches (3.5 cm)
Three-lined pencilfish (*Nannostomus trifasciatus*),
2.2 inches (5.5 cm)

Brood-tending *Lebiasinidae*

Red-spotted Copeina (*Copenia guttata*), 2.8 – 6
inches (7–15 cm)
Origin. Amazon basin.
Habitat. Small bodies of water.
Sexual differences. Female is fatter than the male;
in the male the upper part of the tail fin is more
extended.
Maintenance tank. Species tank. Size: side length
at least 31¹/₂ inches (80 cm). Equipment: soft tank
bed, thick foliage, tight-fitting tank cover (fish
jump out!).
Water. Temperature: 73.4 to 78.8°F (23 to 26°C).
Hardness: 8 to 15 dH. pH: 6.5 to 7.
Food. Live and dry food of all kinds.

Brood-tending *Lebiasinidae*
Red-spotted copeina (*Copeina guttata*),
2.8-6 inches (7-15 cm)
Splash tetra (*Copella arnoldi*), males 3 inches
(8 cm), females 2.4 inches (6 cm)
Banded pyrrhulina (*Purrhulina vittata*),
2.4 inches (6 cm)
(see illustration page 60)
Pyrrhulina brevis, 3.5 inches (9 cm)
Pyrrhulina rachowiana, 2 inches (5 cm)

Reproduction and Rearing
Place the pair in a breeding tank. After spawning,
take out the female—the male alone tends the
brood. When the young emerge, remove the male,
otherwise he'll eat them.

Breeding tank. Capacity: at least 26 gallons (100
liters). Equipment: soft tank bed of fine sand; a
couple of big, flat stones; foliage possible.
Water. Temperature: 75.2 to 82.4°F (24 to 28°C)
Hardness: 6 to 12 dH. pH: 6 to 6.8.
Reproductive behavior. The fish spawn while
circling each other near the stones or on the tank
floor. If they circle in the sand, a spawning pit is
produced, and the eggs cling to each other. After
spawning the male chases away the female,
defends his territory, fans fresh water to the eggs,
and watches over them until the young emerge.
During this time feed sparingly with washed white
worms.
Spawn. Depending on the size of the fish between
160 and 2500 eggs.
Emergence of the young. After 24 to 28 hours; the
fry become free-swimming four days after their
emergence.
Rearing. First food: cleaned paramecia, euglena,
and rotifers; after about a week feed them *Artemia*
and *Cyclops* (feed abundantly). Rearing as with
other characins (see page 71).

Banded Pyrrhulina
(*Pyrrhulina vittata*), 2.4 inches (6 cm)
(see illustration, page 60).
Origin. South America.
Habitat. Small bodies of water.
Sexual differences. Females fatter than males.
Males have red belly and anal fin at spawning time.
Maintenance tank. Species community aquarium.
Size: length of side at least 24 inches (60 cm).
Equipment: the same as for genuine American
characins (see page 79).
Water. Temperature: 71.6 to 77°F (22 to 25°C)
Hardness: 6 to 15 dH (or more). pH: 6 to 7 (filter
with peat).
Food. Live and dry food of all kinds. Insect larvae
promote spawning.

Breeding Instructions for Aquarium Fish

Reproduction and Rearing

Transfer the breeding pair into a breeding tank. After spawning, remove the female—the male cares for the brood. Transfer the male to the maintenance tank once the fry are free-swimming.

Breeding tank. Capacity: 5¼ gallons (20 liters). Equipment: clean, dark sand for tank bed; thick foliage, *Cryptocoryne* or *Echinodorus* plants for egg laying.

Water. Temperature: 75 to 78.8° F (24 to 26° C). Hardness: 6 to 10 dH (and more). pH: 6.5 (filter with peat).

Reproductive behavior. The male polishes a large plant leaf near the water surface and lures the female with fin spreading and body shaking. When she follows him onto the leaf, the fish press together sideways, and the male places his anal fin under the female. He then gathers up the eggs, fertilizes them and lets them drift onto the leaf (to which the eggs adhere). After spawning, the male chases away the female, fans the eggs, and often removes the dead eggs. He guards the eggs and the larvae until the fry swim independently. During this period feed the male sparingly with washed white worms.

Spawn. Up to 150 eggs, (usually less).

Emergence of the young. After about 30 hours; five days after emergence they swim independently.

Rearing. First food: cleaned paramecia and small *cyclops* larvae; afer a week feed with *Artemia* (brine shrimp).

Breeding suggestion: All Pyrrhulina species are bred in the same manner as the banded pyrrhulina.

Splash Tetra (*Copella arnoldi*), males 3.2 inches (8 cm), females 2.4 inches (6 cm).

Origin. Guyana.

Habitat. Small bodies of water.

Sexual differences. Males are more colorful and larger with longer fins; females are fatter.

Maintenance tank. Species or community tank. Size: side length at least 27½ inches (70 cm). Equipment: floor dark if possible; a few dense plant clusters as hiding places; a plant with floating leaves (*Nymphaea*); bright sunlight; tank cover, (fish can leap out).

Water. Temperature: 73.4 to 78.8°F (23 to 26°C). Hardness: 6 to 15 dH. pH: 6.5 to 7.5. (filter with peat).

Food. Living and dry food of all kinds. Insect larvae preferred.

Reproduction and Rearing

Transfer the pair into a breeding tank. Frequently they will spawn in the maintenance tank. Males and females can remain in the breeding tank until the emergence of the young.

Breeding tanks. Capacity: 5¼ gallons (20 liters). Equipment: tank bed and foliage optional. Important: Cover the tank with a frosted glass pane, with the rough side facing the water (so that the fish can cling to it better). The distance from the water surface should be about 2 inches (5 cm). As an alternative, use a piece of green glass or a dark paint spot on the outside of the tank cover to stimulate a leaf.

Water. Temperature: 77 to 80.1°F (25 to 27°C). Hardness: 2 to 12 dH. pH: 6.5 to 7 (filter with peat).

Reproductive behavior. Splash tetras spawn above the water surface, (in the wild probably on a river bank or a large plant leaf sticking out of the water). Both partners leap—tightly pressed to each other—out of the water and, for a moment, press their belly and breast fins and lower jaws tightly against the tank cover. The female sticks a few eggs onto the cover and falls back; the male impregnates them and falls after the female back into the water. They repeat this process over and over. In this way over 150 eggs can be fertilized.

The male remains with the spawn for about 2 days; every now and then he sprays water on the eggs with his tail fin. After emerging, the embryos are washed into the water in this way. The tank cover must fit tightly; the eggs are sensitive to drafts.

Spawn. Mostly 50 to 80 eggs, occasionally up to 150.

Emergence of the young. After about 24 to 30 hours; the fry become free-swimming three days after emergence.

Rearing. First food: cleaned paramecia and euglena; after 8 to 11 days feed them *Artemia* (brine shrimp).

Breeding Instructions for Aquarium Fish

Breeding suggestion: Splash tetras can also spawn on the cover of the community tank. Remove the eggs carefully with a razor blade and put them into a small aquarium with a water level of 1½ to 2½ inches (4 to 6 cm). The water quality and temperature should be the same as in the maintenance tank. The eggs also develop under water.

African Characins
(Alestidae)

The only species of this family that is regularly raised in an aquarium is the Congo tetra.

Congo tetra
(Phenacogrammus interruptus), male 3–4 inches (8.5 cm), female 2.4 inches (6 cm).
Origin. Central Africa.
Habitat. Flowing and stagnant water.
Sexual differences. Male larger than female, with longer, extended rear and anal fins.
Maintenance tank. Species or community aquarium. Size: side length at least 3½ inches (80 cm). Equipment: dark tank bed, thick foliage in the background and on the sides, plenty of swimming room in the middle; floating plants to dim the light.
Water. Temperature: 75 to 81.5°F (24 to 27°C). Hardness: 6 to 15 dH; CH (carbonate hardness) as low as possible. pH: 6.2 to 6.8 (filter with peat). Regular water change (the fish are sensitive to nitrite and nitrates).
Food. Live food of all kinds, especially insect larvae and water fleas; also dry food and plant flakes. (Delicate plants and young sprouts in the aquarium are also eaten.)

Reproduction and Rearing
Begin breeding in early summer (in the wild the spawning time occurs in May and June). Congo tetras spawn in a group rather than in pairs; therefore, if possible place three to four pairs into a larger breeding tank. The spawning period lasts about a week. When well fed the parents hardly bother the eggs. If they do, suck away the eggs carefully and transfer them into a rearing tank about 5¼ gallons (20 liters) in volume.

Breeding tank. Side length at least 31½ inches (80 cm). Equipment: spawning grate not absolutely necessary. Provide robust spawning plants (for example, *Hygrophila* species). Darkening is not necessary, but fish are sensitive to disturbances from the outside.
Water. Temperature: 73.4 to 77°F (23 to 25°C). Hardness: If possible under 3 dH, only with low carbonate level. pH: 6.2 to 6.5 (ample filtering with peat).
Reproductive behavior. The same as with American characins (see page 71). In the beginning the school engages in animated mating. The eggs are released among the plants and fall to the ground.
Spawn. Includes up to 100 eggs a day. The spawning period lasts about a week.
Emergence of the young. After about six days. Since the eggs are not deposited at one time, the oldest of the fry emerge about a week before the youngest. In feeding, therefore, pay attention to the different size classes of the live food (see page 41).
Rearing. First food: cleaned paramecia and rotifers; *Artemia* (brine shrimp) a week later.
Food. Live food of all kinds, especially insect larvae and water fleas; also dry food and plant flakes.

Barbs and Other Cyprinids
(Cypriniformes)

The order *Cypriniformes* embraces over 1400 species. Many, mostly small tropical school fish, can be kept well and reared in aquariums. They are typical school fish that can be kept and bred in species tanks over a long period of time. The most popular barbs—of the genus *Barbus* (see page 80)—and rasboras of the genus *Brachydanio*—of the genera *Danio* (see page 81) and *Rasbora* (see page 85)—are described below.

Breeding Instructions for Aquarium Fish

Barbs
(Genus *Barbus* or *Punitus*)

Barbs can be differentiated into delicate and more robust species (see table of the right). The eggs and larvae of delicate species are very sensitive to infursorians, bacteria, fungi, and dirty water.

Origin. Southern and Southeast Asia, West Africa.

Habitat. Mainly stagnant or slowly flowing waters; many species also in cold, swiftly flowing mountain brooks.

Sexual differences. Females are fatter and stronger; males often are more intensively colored. Some species (for example, the black ruby barb) develop very bright colors at spawning time. Many others develop little white bumps on the head and/or little whittish warts, the so-called spawning rash (most strongly pronounced in males).

Maintenance tank. Species or community aquarium. Size: side length of 24 inches (60 cm) for smaller Barb species (maximum 1.9 inches [5 cm] in length) and at least 31 1/2 inches (80 cm) for larger species. Equipment: fine gravel for tank bed, dark if possible; thick side and background foliage and plenty of open space for swimming; loose, floating surface plants recommended. Not too many fine-leaved plants since most species eat them. Powerful filters.

Water. Temperature: 68 to 78.8°F (20 to 26°C). Hardness and acidity: the hardy species thrive in practically any tap water (10 to over 25 dH), pH about 7. For the delicate species (mostly from the tropical forest regions), use medium-hard, lightly acidic water with a low carbonate content, (7 to 10 dH), pH about 6.5 (filter with peat). Frequent water changes, especially for voracious species (for example, the tiger or Sumatra barb).

Food. Not fastidious eaters. Live food of appropriate size; all dry food and plant flakes. Live food, especially midge larvae, promote spawning. Too plentiful feeding with white worms leads to fatty degeneration and to difficulties in spawning.

Barbs
Arulius barb (*Barbus arulius*)
4.7 inches (12 cm), India
* *Barbus barilioides*
1.9 inches (5 cm), Africa
* *Barbus bimaculatus*
2.8 inches (7 cm), Sri Lanka
Rosy barb (*Barbus conchonius*)
2.4-3.5 inches (6-9 cm),
(in the wild up to 6 inches [15 cm]), India
Cumming's barb (*Barbus cumingi*)
1.9 inches (5 cm), Sir Lanka
Clown barb (*Barbus everetti*)
4-7 inches (12 cm), Southeast Asia
Barbus gelius
1.6 inches (4 cm), India
Barbus jae
1.6 inches (4 cm), Africa
"T" barb (*Barbus lateristriga*)
7.1 inches (18 cm), Southeast Asia
* Striped barb (*Barbus lineatus*)
4.7 inches (12 cm), Malaysia and Indonesia
Black ruby barb (*Barbus nigrofasciatus*)
1.9-2.4 inches (5-6 cm), Sri Lanka
Checkered barb (*Barbus oligolepis*)
1.9-2.4 inches (5-6 cm), Sumatra (see illustration, page 58)
* *Barbus pentazona hexazona*
1.9 inches (5 cm), Southeast Asia
Dwarf barb (*Barbus phutinio*)
1.9 inches (5 cm), Southeast Asia
Schubert's barb (*Barbus semifasciolatus*)
3.9 inches (10 cm), Southeast China
* Tiger or Sumatra barb (*Barbus tetrazona tetrazona*) 2.8 inches (7 cm), Indonesia
(see illustration page 13)
tick tack toe barb (Barbus ticto ticto)
3.9 inches (10 cm), India
Stoliczka's barb (*Barbus ticto stoliczkanus*)
2.4 inches (6 cm), Southeast Asia
* Cherry barb (*Barbus titteya*)
1.9 inches (5 cm), Sri Lanka
* Delicate species whose spawn and larvae are especially sensitive to infusorians bacteria, fungi, and dirty water.

Reproduction and Rearing
Place fish in pairs in the breeding tank. With lively species (for example, rosy barbs) it is better to join one male to two females. Immediately after

spawning put back the parents into the maintenance tank, because most species are avid egg eaters.

Breeding suggestion: If you put the fish into the breeding tank in the evening, they will usually spawn the next morning. The hardier species can be fed a few adult white worms. It is best to put the female into the breeding tank a few hours (or a day) before the male. She can then get used to it and find the hiding places into which she may have to retreat.

Breeding tank. Capacity: 4 gallons (15 liters) for species up to 1.6 inches (4 cm) long; 6 gallons (25 liters) for species up to 4.7 inches (12 cm) long or for very lively fish (for example, the Sumatra barb); 52 gallons (200 liters) for species over 4.7 inches (12 cm) long. Equipment: no tank bed but big pebbles, glass marbles, or spawing grate for protection of the eggs. many dense, fine-leaved plants through which the fish can swim while spawning (the eggs remain hanging). For the sensitive *Barbus* species, disinfect the pebbles and plants (see page 67).

Water. Temperature: 75 to 78.8°F (24 to 26°C) for most species; 78.8 to 82.4°F (26 to 28°C) is desirable for fish such as the clown barbs, cherry barb, and striped barb. Rosy barbs, half-striped barbs, ticktacktoe barbs, and dwarf barbs spawn at 71.6 to 77°F (22 to 25°C). Hardness and acidity: for hardy species the water hardness is almost meaningless; in water of over 15 dH the carbonate level should not be too high; pH about 7. The delicate species are bred in water from 1 to 5 dH, pH 5.5 to 6 (peat filtering).

Reproductive behavior. Barbs are free spawners, and their actual mating is over quickly. The partners press close to each other while swimming and deposit eggs and sperm. With many barb species (for example, the Sumatra barb; see illustration, page 13) the male embraces the female from above and places his tail over her. The eggs are deposited among the plants and fall to the ground.

Spawn. Differs for each species: 40 to 60 eggs for some species, 70 to 100 for others, and about 500 for Sumatra barbs.

Emergence of the young. From 24 to 45 hours, depending on the species; fry swim freely 3 to 4 days after emergence.

Rearing. First food: the fry eat everything they can manage: very fine dry food, or *Cyclops, Diaptoms,* and *Artemia* larvae (except for Cumming's barb). The preferred food for delicate species is *Artemia,* since it does not introduce infusorians into the water. After four to seven days the fry can also eat eel worms; when they reach a length of 0.31 to 0.47 inches (8 to 12 mm), they can also eat plant flakes.

Note. Young barbs often grow in stages; for a while they stay the same, then they grow so rapidly that one can almost see the increase in size. After three or four weeks they can be placed into other aquariums with the same temperature and the same water quality.

Breeding tip: The eggs of barbs are not as sensitive to light as those of most characins. Nevertheless, avoid glaring lights. For delicate species, darken the tank slightly with a newspaper.

Danios
(Brachydanio and Danio)

Origin. South and Southeast Asia.
Habitat. Sunny rivers, brooks, small bodies of water of all kinds, also rice fields.
Sexual differences. Females are plumper than males; males of the genus *Brachydanio* are especially thin.

Danios (Brachydanio and Danio)
Pearl danio (*Brachydanio albolineatus*)
2.4 inches (6 cm), Southeast Asia
Kerr's danio (*Brachydanio kerri*)
1.9 inches (5 cm), Thailand
Spotted danio (*Brachydanio nigrofasciatus*)
1.8 inches (4.5 cm), Burma
Zebra danio or striped danio (*Brachydanio rerio*)
2.4 inches (6 cm), India (see photo, page 120)
Giant danio (*Danio aequipinnatus*)
3.9 inches (10 cm), India, Sri Lanka
Danio devario
6 inches (15 cm), India

Maintenance tank. Species or community aquarium. Size: length of side at least 24 to 32 inches (60 to 80 cm). Equipment: same as for barbs (see page 80).
Water. Temperature: 68 to 75°F (20 to 24°C). Hardness and acidity: 25 dH or more; pH about 7 (as with hardy barbs; see page 80).
Food. As with *Barbus* species (see page 80).

Reproduction and Rearing
Place fish in pairs (or one male with two females) into the breeding tank (the females a day before the male). After spawning remove the parent fish from the tank (egg eaters).
Breeding tank. Capacity: 6½ to 16 gallons (25 to 60 liters) for small species (such as the zebra danio; see photo, page 120), 52 gallons (200 liters) for large and/or productive species (such as the giant danio). Equipment: tank bed of fine sand, preferably pebbles or glass marbles. *Myriphyllum* or *Cabomba* clusters tied together at the top. (In spawning the fish swim through these, and the eggs remain hanging to the plants.) The water level above the plants should not be more than 6 inches (15 cm), so that the eggs can quickly be hidden in the plant clusters. Disinfection of the breeding tank and the equipment is not necessary.
Water. Temperature: 71.6 to 77°F (22 to 25°C). Water quality: as with the hardy barbs (see page 80).
Reproductive behavior. The fish spawn in the morning. The male chases the female furiously. During mating the partners press together closely while swimming and deposit eggs and sperm. The fish eat their eggs; therefore remove the parents immediately after spawning.
Spawn. Between 200 and 500 eggs, depending on the species; the giant danio deposits over 1,000 eggs.
Emergence of the young. After about 90 hours; fry swim freely after three to four days.
Rearing. *Artemia* larvae, infusorians.

Breeding suggestion: *Brachydanio* and *Danio* species can also be bred in an especially equipped aquarium in which several males and females of a species can be kept over a long period of time. With good food they spawn regularly. The fry are nourished by microorganisms, leftover food of the parents, and rearing food such as *Artemia* larvae. The ages of the fry in the breeding tank will differ. As they get older, they are removed from the breeding tank and transferred to a rearing tank.
Breeding tank. Size: length of side 32 inches (80 cm) for eight or more fish.
Equipment. A tank bed of glass marbles or pebbles in the front half of the tanks, sectioned off from the rear part with a glass pane about 4 inches (10 cm) high (glue with silicon rubber). Fill the rear part with a regular tank bed and fine-leaved species suited to the water conditions. Use a powerful filter, and change the water regularly. Temperature and water quality as above.
Caution. In such tanks neither slugs nor Planaria should be permitted to settle, since they would eat the eggs. Even *Cyclops* larvae should not be prepared as food, because the adult *Cyclops* that develop from the uneaten larvae can eat the newly hatched young.

Rainbow Fish
Most rainbow fish mate in the morning. The males then display their splendid mating colors, which fade in the afternoon.
Above: Boeseman's rainbow fish (*Melanotaenia boesemaini*) male in front of the female.
Below: With salmon red rainbow fish (*Glossolepis incisus*), only the biggest fish in the aquarium (and presumably also the dominant male) is a deep salmon red.

Breeding Instructions for Aquarium Fish

Rasbora Species

Species whose eggs are highly sensitive to light are identified in the table at right with an asterisk.
Origin. Southeast Asia.
Habitat. Mostly small bodies of water in the rain forest regions ("black-water" type).
Sexual differences. Females somewhat plumper than the males. Males are often more intensely colored.
Maintenance tank. Species or community tank. Size: side length of 12 inches (30 cm) of side for species up to 1.4 inches (3.5 cm) in length, 24 inches (60 cm) for species up to 1.9 inches (5 cm) in length; and 32 inches (80 cm) or more for larger species. Equipment: the same as for barbs (see page 80); additional floating plants to dim the light.
Water. Temperature: 73.4 to 80.1°F (23 to 27°C). Hardness: 6 to 10 dH; lowest carbonaate level. pH: 6.5 (peat filtering).
Food. Same as for barbs (see page 80). Midge larvae and *Drosophila* (fruit flies) are especially recommended.

Rasbora Species
Red-tailed rasbora (*Rasbora borapetensis*)
1.9 inches (5 cm), Southeast Asia
* Hengel's rasbora (*Rasbora hengeli*)
1.4 inches (3.5 cm), Indonesia
* Harlequin fish (*Rasbora heteromorpha*)
1.8 inches (4.5 cm), Southeast Asia
* Dwarf or spotted rasbora (*Rasbora maculata*)
1 inch (2.5 cm), Southeast Asia
Red-line rasbora (*Rasbora pauciperforata*)
2.8 inches (7 cm), Southeast Asia
Three-lined rasbora or scissortail
      (*Rasbora trilineata*)
6 inches (15 cm), Southeast Asia
* Ocellated dwarf rasbora (*Rasbora urophthalma*)
1.4 inches (3.5 cm), Indonesia
* Ceylonese fire barb (*Rasbora vaterifloris*)
1.6 inches (4 cm), Sri Lanka
* Species with a spawn very sensitive to light.

Reproduction and Rearing

If possible use a pair that have already mated with each other in the maintenance tank. With some fish it is best to pair a year-old female with a male 1¹/₂ to 2 years old. After spawning, put the parents back into the maintenance tank (egg eaters; see page 52).
Breeding tank. Capacity: 4 gallons (15 liters) for species up to 1.2 inches (3 cm) in length; 6¹/₂ gallons (25 liters) for species up to 2 inches (5 cm). in length; 15³/₄ to 21 gallons (60 to 80 liters) for larger species. Equipment: no tank bed, spawning grate is necessary (egg eaters). Anchor down bunches of fine-leaved plants with glass rods. For Hengel's rasbora anchor in the middle of the tank *Cryptocoryne* or another broad-leaved plant. These species lay their eggs on the underside of larger plant leaves. For species with spawn sensitive to light, darken the tank with paper. Since the eggs and fry are susceptible to infusorians, disinfect the tank and equipment before starting to breed (see page 67).
Water. Temperature: 78.8 to 82.4°F (26 to 28°C); 71.6 to 77°F (22 to 25°C) for the ocellated dwarf rasbora. Hardness and acidity: 5 to 12 dH (best at 6 dH; pH between 6 and 7). Barbs with spawn sensitive to light require water of 2 to 5 degrees dH, pH 5.3 to 6, and peat filtering.

Live-bearing toothed carp.
The female of live-bearing toothed carp carries the developing embryos in her body. This requires that she be fertilized internally by the male. For this purpose the anal fin of the male is transformed into a reproductive organ—the so-called gonopodium. Here you see the rarer species *Phallichthys pittieri* (the male on top).

Breeding Instructions for Aquarium Fish

Reproductive behavior. Free spawners with short mating period. With most species the male embraces the female and lays his tail over hers. Hengel's Barb rasboras and harlequin fish stick their eggs under very large plant leaves. The female turns on her back and is embraced by the male, who is also on his back.

Spawn. About 40 eggs for the red-tailed rasbora; other species are more productive.

Emergence of the young. After 24 to 45 hours for most species; the fry swim freely three to four days after emergence.

Rearing. First food: The fry of species under 1 1/2 inches (4 cm) must be fed during the first days with Mardel's Aquarium growth food, cleaned paramecia, or euglena; fry of larger species can be fed *Artemia* (brine shrimp) larvae. Caution: the water may become cloudy with too much rich feeding. After feeding suck up the uneaten food. After three to four weeks the fry can be put into other aquariums (same temperature and water conditions).

Catfish
(Siluriformes)

The order of catfish embraces some 15 families with well over 1000 species. For breeding purposes the following families are of interest:
• Callichthyd and armored catfish, (*Callichthyidae;* see page 86), including callichthyd catfish of the genera *Callichtys, Dianema,* and *Hoplosternum* and armored catfish of the genus *Corydoras*
• Sucker-mouth armored catfish (*Loricariidae;* see page 88).
• Upside-down catfish (*Mochocidae;* see page 93).

Breeding Suggestion: Do not catch larger catfish with the nets in commercial usage; instead, use containers or a coarse threaded fish net (available in bait shops). In finely meshed nets they can get hooked by their fin spines, so that the nets must be cut in order to free them. Injuries from breast and back fin spines of many catfish can cause allergic reactions in people.

Callichthyd and Armored Catfish
(Callichthyidae)

The family *Callichthyidae* embraces catfish of the genera *Callichthys, Dianema,* and *Hoplosternum* as well as armored catfish of the genera *Aspidoras, Brochis,* and *Corydoras.* Representatives of all the genera are bred in the aquarium, especially those of the genus the *Corydoras* (see page 87).

Callichthyd Catfish
(Genera *Callichthys, Dianema, Hoplosternum*). The fish of these genera (see table) reproduce in a very similar manner.

Origin. South America.

Habitat. Flowing and stagnant water with a soft bed and hiding places.

Sexual differences. Males have stronger breast fin spines (genera *Callichthys* and *Hoplosternum*). Females of the genus *Dianema* are plumper at spawning time.

Callichthyd Catfish
Armored catfish (*Callichthys callichthys*), 3.2 inches (8 cm)
Port Hoplo or Atipa catfish (*Hoplosternum thoracatum*), 7.9 inches (20 cm)
Dianema longibarbis, 3.9 inches (9 cm)

Maintenance tanks. Species aquarium; community tank possible. Size: side length at least 32 inches (80 cm). Equipment: soft tank bed; many hiding places in caves and under roots.

Water. Temperature: 77 to 80.1°F (25 to 27°C). Hardness and acidity: water hardness plays no role with *Callichthys* and *Hoplosternum* species (up to 30 dH is tolerated; the carbonate level should not be too high); pH 5.8 to 8.3. For *Dianema* species, which are more sensitive, hardness should not exceed 20 dH: pH 5.5 to 7.5. The fish are also sensitive to nitrate.

Food. Live food of all kinds, dry food, food tablets. Insect larvae, especially red midge larvae, promote spawning.

Breeding Instructions for Aquarium Fish

Reproduction and Rearing

Normally catfish spawn in the species tank. The water level can be lowered by about 8 inches (20 cm). A large leaf on the water surface (*Aspidistra*, philodendron) or a dark, striped styrofoam plate about 4 inches (10 cm) in diameter serve as a roof and support for the male in building the foam nest. After spawning, the male usually chases away the female (therefore, take her out). Once the male finishes tending the brood, remove him too. If you are not especially interested in the brood tending behavior of the male, scoop out the whole nest on the second or third day after spawning (use a soup spoon or a flat bowl) and transfer it into a rearing tank, since the male often eats the young shortly before they leave the nest.

Rearing tanks. Capacity: 2½ to 5¼ gallons (10 to 20 liters) Equipment: no tank bed for better control of the young; aeration with a fine-pored airstone. Distribute large broods after a few days into several tanks with a capacity of about 13 gallons (50 liters); the young ones then grow more uniformly.

Water. Temperature: 78.8 to 82.4°F (26 to 28°C). Hardness and acidity: 10 to 20 dH; pH about 7. Addition of methylene blue or trypaflavine hinders fungal growth on the eggs (see page 68). Draw off about 20 percent of the water once or twice daily, and carefully suck up the uneaten food. Fill the tank with water mixed with methylene blue or trypaflavine.

Reproductive behavior. The male builds a foam nest, by taking air bubbles into his mouth, covering them with saliva, and then spitting them out toward the leaf or styrofoam plate. The nest can be about 1.2 inches (3 cm) high. *Hoplosternum* males also include plant parts in their nest. After a short mating period, during which the male touches the female on the belly and fastens himself to her with his pectoral fin, the female lets a few eggs fall between his pelvic fins, which are folded together to form a pocket, and pastes the eggs onto the nesting roof. After spawning, the male chases out the female (remove the female), guards the nest, and continues to reinforce the foam nest.

Spawn. About 300 to 400 eggs, often more.

Emergence of the young. After four or five days; the fry swim freely a day after emerging.

Rearing. First food: *Artemia* (brine shrimp) larvae, rotifers, fine dry food and chilled *Cyclops* larvae; finely grated egg white can also be used. After two weeks the fry can be fed chopped, washed *Tubifex*, eel worms, small *Cyclops*, and other pond food.

Warning. Keep the rearing tanks clean. No bacterial colonies should be allowed to form on the tank bed or the walls. The young die quickly if they are in contact with bacterial cultures.

Breeding suggestion: Fish prefer to spawn during falling atmospheric pressures (storms). To induce spawning, imitate a storm (rain) and lower the temperature by about 3.5 to 5.5°F (2 to 3°C.)

Armored Catfish (*Corydoras* Species*)*

The most frequently bred species are designated in the table (below) by an asterisk.

Origin. South America.

Habitat. Running and stagnant waters.

Sexual differences. Females are larger and considerably plumper than the males.

Armored Catfish
* Bronze catfish (*Corydoras aeneus*), 2.8 inches (7 cm) (see illustration page 14)
Corydoras barbatus, 4.7 inches (12 cm) Dwarf catfish (*Corydoras hastatus*), 1.2 inches (3 cm)
* Peppered catfish (*Corydoras paleatus*), 2.8 inches (7 cm)
Pigmy catfish (*Corydoras pygmaeus*), 1.2 inches (3 cm)
Rabaut's catfish (*Corydoras rabauti*), 2.4 inches (6 cm)
* Especially frequently bred species.

Maintenance tank. Species or community tank. Size: side length of at least 19½ inches (50 cm). Equipment: soft tank bed; roots, stones, coconut shells, and flowerpots as hiding places. Dense border and background foliage; floating plants for dimming the light.

Breeding Instructions for Aquarium Fish

Water. Temperature: 77 to 80.1°F (25 to 27°C); 73.4°F (73°C) for the peppered and bronze catfish. Hardness and acidity: about 6 dH, pH 6 to 7; many species tolerate even harder water.
Food. See callichthyd catfish, page 86.

Reproduction and Rearing

Armored catfish normally spawn in the species tank when the temperature is raised. Cut off the plant leaves on which the eggs were deposited and transfer them (in a jar filled with aquarium water) into a small rearing tank.
Breeding tank. Size and equipment is the same as for the maintenance tank.
Water. Temperature 80.1 to 86°F (27 to 30°C); 77 to 78°F(25 to 26°C) for bronze and peppered catfish. Hardness: about 6 dH; at a low carbonate level many species spawn even in harder water. For species from tropical forest waters, about 3 dH.
Rearing tank. Capacity: $2^3/_4$ to $5^1/_4$ gallons (10 to 20 liters) Equipment: nothing except a fine airstone.
Water. Same as for the breeding tank. The water is mixed with methylene blue so that the eggs can still be seen. Once or twice daily draw off about 80 percent of the water and refill with lukewarm fresh water and methylene blue.
Reproductive behavior. Armored catfish spawn in groups (in pairs only if necessary); every female needs two or three males. When the females begin to swim around restlessly, they are pursued by the males. Apparently they secrete a scent. During mating a male attaches himself to the female with a pectoral fin, and the animals pull each other through the tank. Often a second male—or even a third one—attaches himself to a fin of the female or of the male. He or they then exude sperm. The female lays one or more eggs and gathers them up with the belly fins folded into a pocket. When the male(s) let(s) go of the female, she swims through the cloud of sperm, and the eggs are fertilized. The female then polishes a leaf, a stone, or a piece of the aquarium pane (it differs from species to species and individually) and pastes the eggs on the cleansed surface.

Breeding suggestion: During the pauses in spawning, the fish sometimes eat their eggs; therefore feed them white worms or *Tubifex.* Eggs that were stuck to the pane are lifted carefully with a razor blade and pasted again in the rearing tank. You can also loosen the eggs with a fingernail. Some experts recommend leaning small glass plates obliquely against the walls of the aquarium. The catfish spawn there and the spawn is removed without difficulty.
Spawn. Between 20 and 100 eggs, depending on the species.
Emergence of the young. After five to six days; two days later they swim freely. After their emergence they look like typewriter commas and at first stay on the ground.
Rearing. First food: rotifers or paramecia, *Artemia,* and *Cyclops* larvae, several days later the fry can eat vinegar eels and fine dry food. After about two weeks they can have finely chopped and washed *Tubifex,* other chopped worms and insect larvae, small *Cyclops* and other pond food. During their first days, dwarf and pigmy catfish fry eat only infusorians.

Breeding suggestion: *Aspidora* and *Brochis* species are bred the same.

Sucker-mouth Armored Catfish
(Loricariidae)

These fish are found mostly in central and northern South America in rapid streams, swift-flowing river, or in large rivers. The overshot mouth has powerful "sucker" lips that help the fish to hold onto the rocks so that they are not carried away by the strong water current. The scraping teeth in the sucker mouth help the fish to scrape off algae. The species or genera (see table on the right) designated by an asterisk are bred regularly; the others are bred less frequently.

Breeding suggestion: Don't use any synthetic fibers for decoration or as filtration material, since the catfish can tear the synthetic material and eat it. Large catfish even tear the insulation off from heating cables and other electrical equipment and thereby cause short circuits. Put such equipment in tubes made of hard PVC (polyvinyl chloride).

Ancistrus species

About 3.9–6 inches (10 to 15 cm) (see photo page 102 and illustrations on page 16 and 45).

Many represented by *Ancistrus dolichopterus*. Similar species, determination is seldom possible.

Origin. Brazil, Amazon tributaries.

Habitat. Brooks, rivers, tropical forest lakes.

Sexual differences. Male has forked tentacles or tentacles divided into 3 parts on the head; female has simple tentacles in a row. At spawning time these are more sharply pronounced.

Maintenance tank. Species or community aquarium. Size: side length of at least 23¹/₂ inches (60 cm). Equipment: large roots as resting places and protective caves. Also caves of stone, coconut shells, and bamboo shoots; tubes of clay or synthetic material through which the fish can pass (about 1.4 to 1.6 inches [3.5 to 4 cm] in diameter). Large-leaved plants and floating plants to dim the light. The fish are active at night; during the day they stay mostly on the underside of the roots.

Water. Temperature: 23 to 27°C. Water quality: 2 to 30 dH, pH-value 5.8 to 7.8. Powerful filtering. Regular water change.

Food. Algae in the aquarium, lettuce, kale, spinach, chickweed, wheat germ (all frozen and thawed so that it is soft enough), thawed frozen peas, live and frozen (thawed) food of all kinds (*Tubifex*, white worms, midge larvae, *Daphnia*, *Cyclops*, mussel meat, and so on). *Ancistrus* species, like all *Loricariidae*, need roughage (cellulose). With their scraping teeth, they scrape around at roots and eat the wood. Feed them in the evenings.

Sucker-mouth armored catfish

* *Ancistrus* species (see above)
  Farlowella species (see page 91)
  Otocinclus species (see page 90)
  Rineloricaria species (see page 90)
  Sturisoma species (see page 92)
  Hypostomus species (see page 92)
* Regularly bred species.

Reproduction and Rearing

Put the male and female pair into the breeding tank; and after the emergence of the young, return them the maintenance tank.

Alternative 1: Breed in the maintenance tank, and raise the young in a rearing container or tank (see Artificial Rearing, page 93).

Alternative 2: Breed in the maintenance tank. Put the male with the spawn into a tube into the rearing tank. Remove after emergence of the young.

Breeding tank. Size: side length of at least 23¹/₂ inches (60 cm). Equipment: no tank bed, otherwise like the maintenance tank. Important: provide spawning caves 1.2 to 1.6 inches (3 to 4 cm) in diameter.

Water. Temperature: 75 to 80.1°F (24 to 27°C). Hardness and acidity: 4 to 10 dH, pH 6.5.

Reproductive behavior. The males build forts around the caves, which they defend against males and frequently against females not ready to spawn. When a female is ready to spawn, she seeks out the male. The fish touch each other with their mouths, then the male leads the female into the cave. After spawning, the male cares for the eggs. In small tanks the female usually is chased away (you should remover her). The male fans fresh water over the clumps of spawn in the cave, pushes them back and forth with his mouth, and rolls them around. When the young emerge, he helps them by sucking the eggshells. He takes care of the young for days at a time after their emergence.

Spawn. Up to 120 eggs, which form a tight clump.

Emergence of the young. After four or five days; they leave the cavern about nine days later and are fed as soon as the yolk sac is consumed.

Rearing. This group is very susceptible to bacteria and infusorians. Water purification is of paramount importance.

Rearing in the breeding tank. The soft rearing food (see page 90) befouls the water in the tank; therefore, exchange at least 80 percent of the tank water for fresh water (same temperature and composition) daily, and suck up the fish droppings.

Rearing in photographic tanks. (see Artificial Rearing, page 93) is less tedious. The water level in the container should be 1.9 inches (5 cm) high. The temperature and water quality should be the same as in the breeding tank. The young are placed daily in containers with freshly prepared water. The old containers must be cleaned thoroughly. *Food*. Provide soft, finely grated or ground plant food, (let stand in flat water dishes in the sun to grow algae); also algae from other tanks; algae powder; baby peas grated or sifted through a sieve; soaked, crushed lettuce leaves and dandelions; chopped and crushed leaves from delicate water plants. In addition, the young ones receive small or chopped and grated live food (for example, rotifers, *Artemia* or *Cyclops* larvae, chopped and rinsed *Tubifex*, sifted through an *Artemia* sieve). They also eat rearing food such as baby brine shrimp and krill and Mandel's Aquarium Growth Food (for plant eaters), crushed food tablets and dry food of all kinds. Feed them in the morning and at night.

Breeding suggestion: Rearing is easiest in a tank with no other fish (temperature and water quality the same as in the rearing tank; slow filters). The young are nourished by algae and microorganisms. Just give a little as a supplement.

Chocolate-colored Catfish
(Rineloricaria lanceolata), 5.1 inches (13 cm)
Origin. Eastern Peru, Amazon drainage area.
Habitat. Brooks, small rivers.
Sexual differences. Males with bristle patches on the sides of the head, the neck region, and the pectoral fins.
Maintenance tank. Species tank or clean community aquarium. Size: side length of at least 23¹/₂ inches (60 cm). Equipment: see page 89.
Water. Temperature: 75 to 82.4°F (24 to 28°C). Hardness and acidity: 2 to 20 dH, pH 5.8 to 7.8. Powerful filter and water current. Perform a partial water change regularly.
Food. See page 89.

Reproduction and Rearing
Breeding management is the same as with *Ancistrus* species (see page 89).
Water. Temperature: 75 to 82.4°F (24 to 28°C). Hardness and acidity: 4 to 10 dH, pH 6 to 6.8.

Reproductive behavior. The male guards and tends the spawn and sucks the young ones during their emergence from the eggshells (see *Ancistrus* species, page 89).
Spawn. Includes about 100 to 150 eggs, (in one hard clump).
Emergence of the young. At 78.8 to 82.4°F (26 to 28°C), after about 9 days; after consuming the yolk sac, the fry are fed.
Rearing. Like the *Ancistrus* species (see page 89) but use *Artemia* larvae as first food; after about a week, feed the fry other rearing food gradually.

Midget Sucker Catfish
(Otocinclus affinis) 1.6 inches (4 cm)
Origin. Southeastern Brazil.
Habitat. Fast-flowing small brooks with clear water, thickly grown with algae and plants.
Sexual differences. Males smaller and thinner than females.
Maintenance tank. Species and community aquarium populated only with small, calm fish. Size: side length of at least 16 inches (42 cm). Equipment: roots as hiding and resting places, dense foliage, easily dimmed light.
Water. Temperature: 71.6 to 78.8°F (22 to 26°C). Hardness and acidity: 2 to 15 dH, pH 5 to 7.5. Clear, well filtered water; regular partial water change. Peat filtering or peat extract supplement if possible.
Food. Algae in the aquarium or on stones (see *Ancistrus* species, page 89) lettuce (soaked or frozen), food tablets, dry food, chopped and rinsed *Tubifex*, white worms, live and thawed water fleas and midge larvae.

Reproduction and Rearing
The fish spawn mostly in maintenance tanks. The breeding pair, however, can also be placed in a breeding tank and, after spawning, can be brought back into the maintenance tank.
Breeding tank. Size and equipment the same as for the maintenance tank (see above).
Water. Temperature: 75 to 78.8°F (24 to 26°C). Other conditions as in the maintenance tank (see above).

Breeding Instructions for Aquarium Fish

Reproductive behavior. The female swims around restlessly, while the male swims around her and mates. The female seeks a spawning place on large-leaved plants. The male prostrates himself before the female, the female adheres tightly to his pelvic fin and sticks three to six eggs onto the leaf (mostly on the underside). The pair can also spawn on the aquarium glass.

Spawn. Can include more than 60 eggs.

Emergence of the young. After two to three days; they get fed as soon as their yolk sac is consumed.

Rearing. Thawed frozen rotifers (if the fry can be placed in an uninhabited aquarium, they will eat the rotifers on the glass), dry food, soaked crushed lettuce. Provide stones or roots overgrown with algae.

Water care. As with *Ancistrus* species (see page 89).

Breeding suggestion: When the fish spawn in the maintenance tank, cut off the leaves on which the eggs were deposited and transfer them to a rearing tank (see Artificial Rearing, page 93)

Needle Catfish

(*Farlowella* species), 6–8 inches (15–20 cm)
Farlowella species are found in the wild in very different biotopes, at different temperatures, and under different water conditions. Temperatures range from 70 to 90°F (21 to 32°C); water hardness from 1 to over 11 dH. Since the fish available in stores usually are imported and often misnamed, you may not know which temperature and water conditions are best for your fish. You must do a little experimenting! With good filtering and ventilation, the fish will tolerate water temperatures about 82.4°F (28°C) and can adjust to a hardness of 17 dH.

Origin. Southern drainage basin of the Amazon.

Habitat. Rivers, pools, flooded ponds.

Sexual differences. Male is thinner, the elongated snout is broader than that of the female; bristles on the snout can get longer and thicker at spawning time.

Maintenance tank. Species tank. Size: side length of at least 32 inches (80 cm). Equipment: prefer-

ably no tank bed (easier to clean). Many roots as hiding places and for nourishment, a few stone disks leaning slantwise against the aquarium walls, large-leaved plants in pots, no bright light! Floating plant roofs possible.

Water. Temperature: 75 to 78.8°F (24 to 26°C). Hardness: 2 to 8 dH. pH: 6 to 7. Peat filtering; efficient filter to keep the water free of nitrogen decomposition products. *Farlowella* species are susceptible to nitrites, nitrates, infusorians, bacteria and heavy metals. The fish droppings must be siphoned off (acidity); the sucked-up water must be replaced by fresh water of the same composition.

Food. The same as for *Ancistrus* species (see page 89). Choose food rich in variety, and feed plentifully. The fish eat at night; therefore, feed them in the evening. During the day fed *Farlowella* can go hungry. (If the fish wander around restlessly and grow thin as rails, they are suffering from hunger.)

Tree roots for scraping are more important for *Farlowella* than for other armored catfish. They can remain alive only if they eat wood as roughage.

Reproduction and Rearing

Put only one pair into the breeding tank for breeding. The males guard their territory and keep weaker males from eating. In order that the male can tend the brood undisturbed, remove the female after spawning.

Breeding tank. Size and installation the same as for the maintenance tank.

Water. Temperature: 70 to 78°F (21 to 26°C). Hardness: 2 to 5 dH. pH: about 6.5. Peat filtering; clean, oxygen-rich water; remove droppings daily.

Reproductive behavior. Clinging closely to each other, the partners clean the spawning bed (aquarium glass) together. Eggs and sperm are emitted while the pair is in close bodily contact. Each mating produces about five eggs, which remain stuck to the pane. Between matings the male swims around, eats, and scrapes wood. Once all the eggs are laid, the male tends the brood. He fans fresh water toward the spawn and helps the young emerge by sucking them out of the egg-shells.

Breeding Instructions for Aquarium Fish

Spawn. Includes about 40 to 60 eggs. These adhere to the glass pane far better in soft water (under 8 dH) than in hard water. In water of 15 dH most of the eggs fall from the pane and must be reared artificially (see page 93).

Emergence of the young. Varies with different broods. At temperatures from 70 to 73.4°F (21 to 23°C) the young of some spawns emerge after 6 or 7 days with a big yolk sac; those of others spawns emerge after 11 days without a yolk sac. (Apparently that is due to the fact that different species were bred). The fry without yolk sacs can be fed immediately; those with yolk sacs are fed only after the consumption of the yolk sacs (also after 11 days).

Rearing. Farlowella fry are even more susceptible to bacteria and infusorians than other armored catfish. They are reared in the manner as *Ancistrus* species.

Food. Like *Ancistrus* species (see page 89). Chopped food on an agar base (see page 59) is least detrimental to the water for sensitive *Farlowella* species. Feed at least twice a day (the fry also eat during the day).

Sturisoma panamense 7.1 inches (18 cm)
Origin. Panama.
Habitat. Fast-flowing waters.
Sexual differences. Male with quills or tentacles on his snout.
Maintenance tank. Species tank (some small, very calm surface fish can be put in). Size: side length of at least 39½ inches (100 cm). Equipment: same as for needle catfish. Cover the tank well, because the fish jump when they are frightened.
Water. Temperature: 68 to 78.8°F (20 to 26°C). Hardness: to 18 dH. pH: 6.5 to 7.2. Powerful filter, strong current, clear water rich in oxygen, peat filtering. Remove fish droppings daily.
Food. As with *Ancistrus* species (see page 89) and needle catfish (see page 91).

Reproduction and Rearing
Breeding management is the same as with needle catfish (above).
Breeding tank. Size and equipment same as with maintenance tank (see above).
Water. Temperature: 75 to 82.4°F (24 to 28°C). Hardness: 2 to 8 dH. pH: 6.5 to 7.
Reproductive behavior. The fish spawn mostly at night, the male alone cleans the spawning area (tank floor or darkest place on the aquarium panes); with other *Sturisoma* species both partners clean. During mating the male places himself diagonally on his side before the head of the female and discharges sperm. The female releases a few eggs, which adhere to the spawning area behind the fish. The male takes care of the brood. He covers the spawn with his body and fans fresh water over it. He is more active in the evening and at night than during the day. Help in emergence is the same as the needle catfish (see page 91).
Spawn. Includes up to 200 eggs; in hard water they fall off the glass pane (see page 91).
Emergence of the young. After six to nine days, depending on the temperature; the fry swim freely after about three days.
Rearing. Same as with needle catfish (see page 91).
Note. The other *Sturisoma* species are bred in the same manner.

Hypostomus **species**
12 inches (over 30 cm)
Origin. South America.
Habitat. Rivers, lakes.
Sexual differences. Unknown.
Maintenance tank. Species or clean community aquarium. Size: side length of at least 47 inches (120 cm). Equipment: the same as for *Ancistrus* species (see page 89); provide caves 4 inches (10 cm) in diameter for the larger fish.
Water. Temperature: 71.6 to 82.3°F (22 to 28°C). Hardness: 1 to 25 dH. pH: 5 to 8.
Food. The same as for *Ancistrus* species (see page 89), but also fish and mammal meat, trout pellets, dog biscuits, dry cat food, shrimp, rolled oats.

Reproduction and Rearing
The breeding regimen is the same as for *Ancistrus* species (see page 89).
Breeding tank. Size: side length of at least 39 inches (100 cm). Equipment: as for *Ancistrus*

species (see page 89).
Water. Temperature: 75 to 78.8°F (24 to 26°C).
Hardness: 2 to 10 dH. pH: 6 to 7.
Reproductive behavior. The fish spawn in caves.
The male holds on with his mouth to the tail region
of the female and stimulates her to spawn by
convulsive body movements. The male tends the
eggs (take the female out of small tanks), fans
them, sucks them, and rolls the spawn clump
around.
Spawn. Includes about 260 eggs.
Emergence of the young. Five days after spawning
(with help of the male); nine days later the fry
begin to eat.
Rearing. Same as for *Ancistrus* species (see page
89).

Artificial Rearing Sucker-mouth Armored Catfish

Otocinclus species do not tend their brood. Even in
brood-tending species the male sometimes does not
tend the brood or begins to eat the eggs. Or, as in
the case of *Farlowella* and *Sturisoma* species, the
eggs may not adhere to the glass pane (in hard
water) and fall to the bottom. In such cases the
eggs must be reared artificially. The spawn is
placed in a small rearing tank or a photographic
developing tank containing about 2 inches (5 cm)
of water (height) and a fine airstone. If the spawn
is in a cave, transfer the spawn with the cave if
possible. Loose eggs of *Sturisoma* and *Farlowella*
species are sucked up with a tube and transferred to
the rearing container. The eggs of *Otocinclus*
species are transferred together with the leaves on
which they are desposited.
Mix the water with methylene blue so that the eggs
can still be seen. Twice a day change about 80
percent of the water for water containing methylene blue. As soon as the young begin to emerge (or
several hours before the expected emergence), suck
up the spawn carefully with a pipe or a thin rubber
tube until the young break out of the eggshells. The
same thing is accomplished if you brush the eggs
gently with a bristle brush.

Upside-Down Catfish
(Mochocidae)

The best known species are the upside-down
catfish (*Synodontis nigriventris*) and the
Synodontis petricola.

Upside-Down Catfish
(Synodontis nigriventris)
Female 3.9 inches (10 cm), Male 3.2 inches (8 cm)
Origin. Africa.
Habitat. Running and stagnant water.
Sexual differences. Females are larger and plumper
than the males.
Maintenance tank. Species or community tanks.
Size: side length of at least 32 inches (80 cm).
Equipment: soft tank bed, large-leaved plants,
caves, hiding places.
Water. Temperature: 75 to 80.1°F (24 to 27°C).
Hardness: 6 dH (low carbonate level). pH: 6.5.
Food. Live food of all kinds, especially insect
larvae and worms. The fish like to swim beneath
the water surface and suck in the gnat larvae
hanging there. Plentiful feeding with black gnat
larvae stimulates spawning.

Reproduction and Rearing
The fish spawn in the maintenance tank (species
tank). They probably can be induced to spawn by
imitating a thunder storm (see pages 66 and 67).
Breeding tank. Unnecessary.
Reproductive behavior. Mating and spawning have
not been closely observed yet.
Spawn is attached to the aquarium panes (100 to
1,000 eggs).
Emergence of the young. At 75°F (24°C), on the
seventh or eighth day; at 80.1°F (27°C) on the
fourth or fifth day. The fry consume their yolk sac
and begin to eat five days after emergence.
Rearing. First food: *Artemia* larvae, rotifers, very
fine *Cyclops* larvae; somewhat later the fry can eat
eel worms. After two to three weeks they can
receive pellets and finely grated dry food. By the
seventh or eighth week, the young begin to swim
on their backs like their parents.

Cuckoo Catfish

(*Synodontis petricola*), 4.7 inches (12 cm)
This catfish, originating in Lake Tanganyika, is one of the most interesting fish ever observed. If you want to breed this species, you must keep it together with mouthbreeding cichlids from the Tanganyika or Malawi lakes.
Origin. Africa (Lake Tanganyika Sea).
Habitat. Rocky shore regions.
Sexual differences. Females ready to spawn are plumper than males.
Maintenance tank. Community tank with mouthbreeding cichlids from Lake Tanganyika. Size: side length of at least 47 inches (120 cm). Equipment: Same as for mouthbreeders from Lake Tanganyika and Lake Malawi (see page 111).
Water. Temperature: 77 to 80.1°F (25 to 27°C). Hardness: 15 to 35 dH. pH: 7.5 to 8.2. The fish are suited to relatively high levels of carbonates (Tanganyika water).
Food. Live food of all kinds, especially insect larvae, worms, and smaller fish.

Reproduction and Rearing

Breeding takes place in the maintenance tank. Water temperature and quality need not be changed. The parents must not be removed after spawning.
Breeding tank. Unnecessary.
Reproductive behavior. Cuckoo catfish ready to spawn lie in wait for mouthbreeders that are just beginning to spawn. As soon as the cichlid female has laid a few eggs in the spawning nest of the male and turns around to take them into her mouth, the catfish quickly dart among the cichlids and scoop up the eggs. The catfish pair mates, and the female deposits several catfish eggs into the nest. The cichlid female unsuspectingly takes them into her mouth and cares for them together with her own "children." The young catfish complete their development in the mouth of the cichlid mother and are protected by her even after they leave her mouth. Such fish have a good chance of survival. In the aquarium this behavior was first observed when cuckoo catfish were kept together with perch of the *Haplochromis* family from Lake Malawi. Since then two other *Synodontis* species have been

discovered (*Synodontis eurystomus* and *Synodontis multipunctatus*) that also parcel out their children to different mouthbreeding species of the *Haplochromis* family.
Spawn. Includes over 20 eggs.
Emergence of the young. The emergence is unknown; after about a month the young are let out of the mouth of the cichlids.
Rearing is undertaken by the cichlids. The catfish fry, like the cichlids, eat *Artemia* larvae and other rearing food. They also eat microorganisms (bacteria, rotifers, protozoa, algae), which are always present in aquariums. Often they will eat their "stepsiblings," which grow more slowly.

Glass Catfish
(*Schilbeidae*)

Eutropiellus vanderweyeri, which has been bred in captivity, is often confused with *Eutropiellus debauwi,* about which no positive breeding data are available.
(*Eutropiellus vanderweyeri*)
3.2 inches (8 cm)
Origin. Africa.
Habitat. Running and stagnant water.
Sexual differences. Females ready to spawn are plumper than males.
Maintenance tank. Species or community tank with calm, gentle fish (for example characins or barbs). Size: side length of at least 39 inches (100 cm). Equipment: same as for characins (see page 71) and barbs (see page 79). Fine-leaved plants, large swimming area, some floating plants. Powerful current by centrifugal pump or motor filter (fish like to stay in the current).
Water. Temperature: 54 to 80.1°F (12 to 27°C). Hardness: up to 18 dH; lowest possible carbonate level. pH: 6.5 to 7.2.
Food. Live food (red and black midge larvae), food flakes, and frozen food.

Reproduction and Rearing

For breeding place two males and one female in the breeding tank. After spawning return the parents to the maintenance tank.

Breeding tank. Size: side length of 24 inches (60 cm). Equipment: no tank bed; fine-plumed spawning plants.
Water. Temperature: 75 to 78.7°F (24 to 26°C). Hardness: 4 to 8 dH. pH: 6 to 7.
Reproductive behavior. The fish spawn mostly in the morning hours. The eggs are strewn among fine-plumed plants.
Spawn. About 100 eggs.
Emergence of the young. After about three days.
Rearing. First food: Infusorians and rotifers, freshly emerged *Artemia* larvae; later the fry can eat frozen and dry food preparations.

Egg-laying Toothed Carp or Killifish (*Cyprinodontidae*)

Fish of the *Cyprinodontidae* family are found in tropical and subtropical regions on all continents except Australia. Geologically it is a relatively young family, and new species are constantly forming. In the aquarium many subspecies and varieties are crossbred since the females of many species strongly resemble each other, and the males mate with females of strange species when sex partners of their own species are not available. Egg-laying toothed carp are divided into two groups, according to their reproductive methods: fish that spawn on the bottom (ground spawners) and those that usually spawn on plants (plant spawners), to which the eggs adhere.

Ground Spawners
Ground spawners are so-called seasonal fish that live in tiny ponds which are filled with water only during the rainy season. During spawning they press their eggs into the ground. Some spawning fish—of the genera *Austrofundulus, Cynolebias,* and *Pterolebias*—submerge themselves completely in the bottom soil (see photo page 37).
During the dry season the ponds dry up, and the adult fish die. But the eggs survive in the mud. In the next rainy season the ponds fill up again, the fry hatch, and the young develop into adults within a few months. They in turn spawn at the end of the rainy season. Therefore, in the wild they live no

more than eight months; even in the aquarium they live at the most only 1 1/2 years.
The development of the eggs is controlled by the oxygen content of the ground. When the ponds are full, bacteria and other micoorganisms in the ground use up oxygen. In this oxygen-poor milieu the eggs develop up to the formation of the yolk sacs (see page 53). When the ponds dry up, the mircroorganisms die. The ground becomes brittle, and the oxygen content rises again. The eggs now begin to develop further, until the embryo is ready to emerge. When the next rainy season begins, microorganisms develop again and multiply, so that the oxygen content of the ground decreases. For the young ones that is the signal for emergence. Glands in their head secrete enzymes which dissolve the eggshell, and differences in osmotic pressure (see page 28) expand the egg so that the young can emerge easily.

Plant Spawners
Plant spawners live in calm waters and deposit their eggs on plants, roots, or in stone crevices. Some also spawn on the ground. The eggs require no dry period to develop. These fish can live for many years in the wild.

Maintenance of Ground and Plant Spawners
Maintenance tank. Preferably a species aquarium. Size: 20 to 24 inches (50 to 60 cm) side length for species under 4 inches (10 cm) in length; 28 inches (70 cm) or more for larger species. Equipment: for ground and plant spawners from tropical rain forest waters and Savanna waters (many members of the genera *Aplochielichthys, Aplocheilus, Cynolebias, Nothobranchius* and *Roloffia*): tank bed of dark, fine, granulated pebbles or boiled peat. Twigs and stones for hiding places (most killifish are territorials, and the females are often pursued). Plants that need little light (for example, *Cryptocorynen, Java fern* and *Java moss*); Floating plants for dimming the light.
Equipment for plant spawners from sunny brooks, desert ponds, and brackish water (members of the genera *Cyprinodon, Aphanius, Fundulus, Rivulus,* and *Oryzias*): tank bed of bright sand or pebbles, hiding places among stones and plants. Water

Breeding Instructions for Aquarium Fish

plants that tolerate hard water (for example, *Sagittaria, Vallisneria, Egeria, Elodea*). Brighter light for plant eating species to promote the growth of algae.

Water. Temperature: 64.4 to 71.6°F (18 to 22°C). for fish from temperate zones (Europe, North America) and from tropical mountain regions (*Epiplatys* and *Aphyosemion* species from the mountains of West Africa, *Cynolebias* species from southern South America); 71.6 to 75°F (22 to 24°C) for other species; 78.8°F (26°C) for seasonal fish; 86°F (30°C). for desert fish, which, however, need a night temperature at least 19°F (10°C) cooler.

Water Composition: Egg-laying killifish have adjusted to very different types of water (tropical forest brooks; rain ponds with very soft and acid water; brackish water at mouths of rivers; medium-hard, neutral to alkaline rivers and seas; and desert ponds and mineral springs with a high salt content). Most species are maintained in water with a hardness of about 8 to 10 dH (often even in harder water). Many killifish are very sensitive to changes in the water composition—especially to changes in pH. The water composition must therefore be carefully monitored. All killifish need clean water; they don't tolerate nitrogen compounds, especially nitrites. Change the water regularly.

Food. In the wild most killifish feed on flying insects and mosquito larvae; therefore, live food is essential. Use dry food only as supplementary nourishment. Well-suited live food includes midge larvae, especially gnat larvae, *Drosophila*, insects of suitable size, and insect larvae. For species from brackish water (see table, page 104) include also water fleas, white worms, and thawed frozen food. North American and southern European species require more algae and other plant food.

Reproduction and Rearing of Ground Spawners
Place a pair or a male with two females in the breeding tank. Most killifish are continual spawners, laying eggs over a long period of time. After 8 to 14 days, take out the fish and drain the water in the tank. Alternatively, separate the males from the females and feed them well for a week;

then pair them again for breeding.

Put the tank bed (peat) in which the eggs have been deposited into a net and squeeze it carefully to remove excess water. Place the eggs with the peat in a plastic container and label it with the name of the fish, the spawning date, and the probable date of emergence. To prevent the formation of mildew, puncture the container or open it occasionally to let in air.

This "dry period" is necessary for the eggs to develop. It varies depending on the species. From time to time take the fish out of the peat (they have hard shells) and see how far the embryos have developed. If the silvery eyes shine through the eggshell, the fish are ready to emerge.

Empty the peat into a flat tray and sprinkle with water at about 68°F (20°C), whose composition corresponds to that of the breeding water. The first fry should emerge after a few hours. If nothing happens after two days, squeeze the peat again to remove the water and store it for an additional two to four weeks. Then repeat the entire process. Even if the young do emerge, the peat must be sprinkled at intervals of two to four weeks, since seasonal fish produce eggs that develop at different rates. If the young ones don't emerge at all (even if they can still be seen in the egg), create a shortage of oxygen (the stimulus for hatching) artificially by blowing exhaled (oxygen-poor) air with a straw into the water or by scattering some dry food on the water surface; this promotes the development of infusorians, which use up oxygen. You can also put the eggshells for a short while into the refrigerator and cool the water to 59 to 61°F (15 to 16°C). Fish out the hatched fry immediately and transfer them to a clean rearing tank (temperature and water quality the same as in the hatching tank).

Breeding suggestion: Moistened peat floats near the water surface. If you crumble it between your fingers, the ripe eggs will fall into the water. The fry are easier to catch if they are not hidden in the peat.

Alternative: You need less peat if you place plastic containers filled with peat into the breeding tank. The fish use them for spawning.

Breeding Instructions for Aquarium Fish

Breeding tank. Capacity: about 3 gallons (12 liters) for fish up to 3.9 inches (10 cm) in length; at least 8 gallons (30 liters) for larger fish. Disinfect the tank before installation. Equipment: for the tank bed a layer of extracted, well-rinsed peat (you can also use crumbly filter peat from the pet shop or garden peat without additives; see Peat Testing page 34). For species that burrow into the ground to spawn, the peat layer must be thicker than the average length of the fish. Also add roots and stones as hiding places for females. A light-fitting tank cover is necessary (the fish leap).

Water. The temperature and composition for individual species are found in the table (see page 98).

Reproductive behavior. See page 95.

Spawn. The number of eggs varies for each species.

Emergence of the young. Length of time for development of the eggs (until emergence hatching):

Large *Aphyosemion* species	3–5 months
Austrofundulus species	4–6 months
Cynolebias species	2-4 months
Nothobranchius species	2–8 months
Rachovia species	2-6 months
Roloffia species	3–6 months

Rearing. The young at emergence are so well developed that they can hunt for their own food. Almost all species eat a few hours after emergence. First food: *Artemia* larvae, paramecia for small species (exception: the extremely small fry of *Epiplatys* and *Pseudepiplatys* species still cannot eat this food. They are reared in the maintenance tank, in which they can be nourished by the microfauna present there.)

Subsequent food: *Cyclops* larvae (just a little), eel worms, later even water fleas and white worms. Ground spawners can eat more white worms than is healthy for other fish. They need very nourishing food, since they reach sexual maturity after five to six weeks.

Breeding suggestion: The rearing tanks for the older fry should be as big as possible. Frequent water changes and good food are essential for them

to grow quickly and uniformly. Species that spawn in soft water and must be reared in soft water should slowly be acclimated to medium-hard water, so that they will not be harmed when they are transferred to other tanks.

Reproduction and Rearing of Plant Spawners

Place a male and a female (with aggressive species, several females and one male) into the breeding tank. Plant spawners (like ground spawners) lay their eggs over an extended period of time. Gather the eggs daily in plastic containers with water from the breeding tank, mixed with trypaflavine or with fresh, chlorine-free water of the same composition. Parents (hardly any eat their eggs) can remain in the breeding tank, until the young begin to emerge. Scoop up the hatched fry, and raise them in a rearing basin. Since the fish lay their eggs over a long period of time, the fry are of different sizes. This means that they must be kept in different rearing tanks and given food in accordance with their size.

Breeding suggestion: The rearing is easier if the eggs are treated like those of the ground spawners (see page 95). Gather the eggs from the tank bed, place them in damp peat, and store them in plastic containers. After two to four weeks add lukewarm breeding water. In this way all the emerged young are of equal age and can be treated equally.

Breeding tank. Size: see table, page 98. Equipment: no tank bed; many fine-plumed plants, such as Java moss, *Cabomba*, or *Myriophyllum*; or long peat fibers that are fastened to the tank cover and hang in the water (they also serve the females as hiding places). A tank cover is necessary because the fish jump.

Water. The temperature and composition for individual species are listed in the table (see page 98).

Reproductive behavior. See page 94.

Spawn. Number of eggs varies according to species.

Emergence of the young. About three weeks after the eggs are deposited.

Rearing. Same as for ground spawners (see page 95).

Breeding Instructions for Aquarium Fish

Breeding suggestion: If you buy imported fish from different localities, put them in separate tanks in order to avoid crossbreeding fish of different varieties and species. Such crossbreeding may produce fertile offspring, but the fertility and vitality of offspring of the next or following generations may decline.

1. Example of a Ground Spawner

Black-finned Pearlfish
(*Cynolebias nigripinnis*), 1.8 inches (4–5 cm).
A popular ground spawner that submerges itself completely during spawning.
Origin. South America (Argentina).

Breeding Data for Popular Killifish: Ground Spawners

Name	Breeding Tank	Water Conditions	Comments ♂=male, ♀=female
Arnold's lyretail *Aphyosemion arnoldi*	3 gallons (12 liters)	71.6–77°F (22–25°C) 2–6 dH, pH 6.5	1 ♂ and 2–3 ♀ for breeding.
Golden pheasant gularis *Aphyosemion sjoestedti*	5¼ gallons (20 liters)	71.6–75°F (22–24°C) 5–10 dH, pH 6.5	in pairs or 1 ♂ with several ♀ for breeding.
Austrofundulus limnaeus	3 gallons (12 liters)	71.6–78.8°F (22–26°C) 3–6 dH, pH 6.5	1 ♂ and 2 ♀ for breeding; tank should not be too bright.
Argentine pearfish *Cynolebias bellotti*	3 gallons (12 liters)	68–77°F (20–25°C) 5 dH, pH 6.5	♂ aggressive at spawning time.
Palmquist's nothobranch *Nothobranchius palmquisti*	3 gallons (12 liters)	71.6–75°F (22–24°C) 5–8 dH, pH 6–6.5	♂ aggressive
Longfin *Pterolebias longipinnis*	5¼ gallons (20 liters)	68–75°F (20–24°C) 5 dH, pH 6.5	♂ aggressive.
Roloffia occidentalis	5¼ gallons (20 liters)	71.6–77°F (22–25°C) 1-6 dH, pH 6-6.5	♂ aggressive: 1 couple or 1 ♂ and 2–3 ♀ for breeding.
Terranatos (Austrofundulus) dolichopterus	3 gallons (12 liters)	75–78.8°F (24–26°C) 2–3 dH, pH 6–6.5	1 ♂ and 2–3 ♀ for breeding; breeding tank not too bright.

Breeding Instructions for Aquarium Fish

Habitat. Small bodies of water with a soft ground, rain puddles.

Sexual differences. Males bigger and more colorful than the females.

Maintenance tanks. Species tank. Size: side length of at least 15³/₄ inches (40 cm). Equipment: soft, dark tank bed; light, fine-plumed plants and twigs for hiding places.

Water. Temperature: 68 to 75°F (20 to 24°C). Hardness: 5 to 8 dH. pH: 6.5 to 7.

Food. Live food of all kinds (see description of families, page 112).

Reproduction and Rearing

Put one pair or one male with two or three females into the breeding tank. After spawning return the fish to the maintenance tank.

Breeding tank. Capacity: about 3 gallons (12 liters). Equipment: for tank bed a peat layer about 3.2 inches (8 cm) thick; some hiding places for the females (see page 97).

Water. Temperature: 71.6 to 75°F (22 to 24°C). Hardness: 3 to 5 dH. pH: 6.5.

Reproductive behavior. During mating the male swims around the female with outspread fins. If the female is ready to spawn, she follows him. The male places himself obliquely or vertically with his head to the ground, the female places herself next to him, and the two, embracing tightly, submerge themselves into the ground and spawn. The male emerges first to the surface.

Spawn. Spawning period lasts over a week; altogether some 150 eggs are deposited. For preservation of the peat with the eggs, see page 96.

Emergence of the young. Sprinkle the peat after 3 months (see page 96).

Rearing. First food: *Artemia* larve.

2. Example of a Ground Spawner

Rachov's Nothobranch

(*Nothobranchius rachovi*), 3.5 inches (9 cm). This species does not submerge completely during spawning.

Origin. Africa (Mozambique).

Habitat. Rain puddles in the Savanna.

Sexual differences. Males larger, brilliantly colored, females dull.

Maintenance tank. Species tank. Size: side length of 35¹/₂ inches (90 cm) or more. Equipment: soft, dark tank bed; twigs; light vegetation.

Water. Temperature: 68 to 73.4°F (20 to 23°C). Hardness: 5 to 8 dH. pH: 6.5. No strong current, but regular water changes (about a fifth of the tank per week).

Food. Live and dry food (see page 41).

Reproduction and Rearing

Place a pair of fish into the breeding tank. After spawning put the fish back into the maintenance tank or another breeding tank. Store the peat (tank bed) with the eggs in a plastic container (see page 96).

Breeding tank. Capacity: about 3 gallons (12 liters). Equipment: tank bed of peat about 1.6 inches (4 cm) thick; some hiding places for the female.

Water. Temperature: 71.6 to 75°F (22 to 24°C). Hardness: 4 to 6 dH. pH: 6.5.

Reproductive behavior is similar to that of the black-finned pearlfish (see above), except that the fish do not submerge themselves completely in the peat. The male seizes the tail end of the female with his rear and anal fins. The female lays one egg, which falls into the cone-formed by her anal fin and there is fertilized by the male. The egg then glides to the ground.

Spawn. Includes about 200 eggs, which are laid over a period of several days. For preservation of the peat with the eggs; see page 96.

Emergence of the young. Sprinkle the peat with water after about 3 months. Soft water (2 dH) produces the best results.

Rearing. First food: *Artemia* larvae.

Breeding Instructions for Aquarium Fish

Example of a Plant Spawner

Lyretail
(*Aphyosemion australe*), 2.2 inches (5.5 cm)
The breeding of this very beautiful killifish is typical for all plant spawners. Fish can also spawn on the ground surface.
Origin. West Africa.
Habitat. Small tropical rain forest waters.
Sexual differences. Males bigger, very beautifully colored, extended tail fin and tips of the rear and anal fins. Females are brownish, with rounder tail fin.
Maintenance tank. Species tank or community tank with small, calm fish. Size: side length of 20 inches (50 cm) or more. Equipment: dark tank bed (for example, a peat layer on pebbles); hiding places of roots and stones; dense side and background foliage; subdued lighting by means of floating plants.
Water. Temperature: 68 to 73°F (21 to 24°C). Hardness: 8 to 10 dH. pH: 5.5 to 6.5. Peat filter.
Food. Live food of all kinds; dry food.

Reproduction and Rearing
Place a pair of fish into the breeding tank and gather the eggs daily (see page 97).
Breeding tank. Capacity: about 3 gallons (12 liters). Equipment: tank bed not necessary, but fine-plumed plants or spawning webs (weighted with glass rods or pebbles).
Water. Temperature: 73.4 to 75.2°F (23 to 24°C). Hardness: about 5 dH. pH: 6.5. Light sea salt supplement: 1 teaspoon to 2.5 gallons (10 liters) of water.
Reproductive behavior. These plant spawners mate with spread fins and "fluttering dances," just like ground spawners. The fish spawn among fine-plumed plants as well as on or in spawning webs. They press against each other, and the female lays an egg, which is hurled toward the spawning bed and remains hanging there by its thread.
Spawn. During a spawning period of about 12 days, 10 to 20 eggs are laid daily (altogether up to 150). Remove them daily from the breeding tank together with the spawning bed, and transfer them to the rearing tank (filled with water from the breeding tank). Alternatively, store the eggs and then spray them, as with ground spawners.
Emergence of the young. After about 14 days.
Rearing. First food: *Artemia* larvae.

Live-bearing Toothed Carp (*Poeciliidae*)

This fish family is native to the New World, from the southern United States down through Central America to northern Argentina. The fish were introduced to other areas, chiefly Southest Asia and the Philippines, to keep in check malarial mosquitoes.

Specialized Biology of Live-bearing Fish
The anal fin of the male is transformed into a movable reproductive organ, the so-called gonopodium. For copulation the gonopodium is extended sideways and, through this U-shaped channel, the male deposits a pocket of sperm into the sexual opening of the female. Only a part of the packet is used to fertilize the mature eggs, the rest is stored in the folds of the fallopian tubes and nourished there by the cellular tissue. Thus new eggs can be fertilized even without the presence of a male (reserve fertilization).

Dwarf gourami couple shortly before spawning.
The males of these labyrinth fish build a foam nest among floating plants from slime-covered air bubbles. Mating and spawning always take place under the nest.

Breeding Instructions for Aquarium Fish

The embryos develop within the female in large eggs, rich in yolk, and break out of the eggs at the time of birth. Thus, strictly speaking, the eggs are "born" (ovoviviparity). But the embryos are also nourished with oxygen and nutrients from the mother. The ovaries are merged into a single organ so that the larvae eggs will have enough room. Only in the mosquitofish (*Heterandria formosa*) is the ovary too small to accommodate the large eggs. Here the young develop sequentially or in small groups. The oldest are born while the youngest are just starting their development, in "conveyor belt" fashion. Live bearing is the most highly developed form of brood tending; the young are protected from enemies and unfavorable environmental conditions right up to birth.

Successful Propagation through Selective Breeding

The popular guppies and platys are available in tropical fish stores in many different varieties. Some species and varieties of live-bearing toothed carp can be crossbred in the aquarium.
• All guppy purebred varieties can be crossbred.
• The guppy wild form can be crossbred with all guppy varieties.

Two of them or just one?
Above: With most cichlids both parents engage in brood tending. If the couple quarrels—as here with *Lamprologus obsxurus*, a cichlid from Lake Tanganyika—then the spawn is in jeopardy. This happens relatively often in the aquarium.
Below: Most brood-tending catfish do not quarrel with their mates, because the male usualy takes over care of the brood. Here you can see sucker-mouth armored catfish male (*Ancistrus* species). The eggs are stuck to the aquarium pane, the male is attached to the pane with his mouth and fans fresh oxygen-rich water to the eggs. He even recognizes unfertilized or dead eggs and eats them. The empty eggshells remain behind (in the picture the whitish one).

• The black molly (*Poecilia sphenops*) can be crossbred with the sailfin molly (*Poecilia velifera*) and *Poecilia latipinna*.
• Wild forms of the platy and the variegated platy, as well as the aquarium-bred forms, can be crossbred.
If you value high quality marketable offspring, you should keep only fish of purebred stock. Otherwise you will get offspring that do not resemble the parents, and the best you can do with these is to give them away to friends.
• Guppy males with fancy fins are often incapable of reproducing as soon as the fins are fully formed. The condition also affects the gonopodium. Therefore they must be started on breeding when they are half grown.
• The same is true of the fancy forms of the platy who are likewise not capable of reproducing. The females are fertilized artificially by means of a pipette.
Since many viviparous carp are able to reproduce at the age of a few weeks or months, the sexes must be separated as soon as one can tell them apart (with guppies by the third week). The rearing basins therefore must be inspected at least once a week. Young males with the gonopodium are taken out right away and raised in male aquariums. For breeding one uses the best animals, that is, those who show next to perfect body shape, fins and coloring, also the most vitality. With many species, however, the breeding creatures should not be chosen too early:
• Males which develop a high rear fin early should not be prepared for breeding. Only males which develop large rear fins after at least a year are strong and of good color and pass on these qualities.
• In some cases there are early males and late males. The early males form their gonopodium after about four to five months, the late males form theirs only after a year and a half and the continuation on the tail fin. Late males therefore are equal to the sexual readiness of the females, the majority however get bigger and more beautiful than the early males. Therefore: Don't sort out "females" which have no young ones and don't prepare them for food! They are late males!

Breeding Instructions for Aquarium Fish

Breeding Data for Popular Killifish: Plant Spawners

Name	Breeding Tank	Water Conditions	Comments ♂=male, ♀=female
Adinia multifasciata	5¼ gallons (20 liters) fresh water with ¼–½ seawater supplement.	71.6°F (About 22°C)	Very aggressive in small tanks without hiding places. Plant food also necessary.
Spanish minnow *Aphanius iberus*	5¼ gallons (20 liters)	86°F (About 30°C) 8-12 dH, pH 7	Keep cool in winter about 53.6–60.8°F (12–16°C). Feed parents well in breeding basin, otherwise they eat eggs.
Aphyosemion bualanum	3 gallons (12 liters)	70–75°F (21–24°C) 2–5 dH, pH 6–6.5	pH not higher than 7.
Aphyosemion exiguum	3 gallons (12 liters)	71.6–77°F (22–25°C) About 5 dH, pH 6–6.5	Maintenance in hard, alkaline water also possible.
Aphyosemion striatum	3 gallons (12 liters)	71.6–75°F (22–24°C) 3–6 dH, pH 6.5	1 teaspoon sea salt per 2½ gallons (10 liters).
Aplocheilichthys spilauchen	5¼ gallons (20 liters)	78.8–86°F (26–30°C) 5–8 dH, pH 6.5	10–15% seawater supplement. Sensitive to infusorians.
Striped panchax *Aplocheilus lineatus*	8 gallons (30 liters)	77–82.4°F (25–28°C) 4–12 dH, pH 6–7	Maintenance only with fish of equal size or larger.
Chevalier's panchax *Epiplatys chevalieri*	5¼ gallons (20 liters)	75–78.8°F (24–26°C) 4–12 dH, pH 6.5	Sea salt supplement desirable. Does not eat its eggs. Sensitive to infusorians.
American flagfish *Jordanella floridae*	5¼ gallons (20 liters)	73.4–77°F (23–25°C) 2–5 dH, pH 6.5–7	Spawn in cavities in sand. ♂ aggressive. Take out ♀ after spawning. Algae and plant food.
Playfair's panchax *Pachypanchax playfairi*	5¼ gallons (20 liters)	75–78.8°F (24–26°C) 5–12 dH, pH 6.5–7	Eats its own eggs.
Pseudepiplatys annulatus	3 gallons (12 liters)	75–78.8°F (24–26°C) 1–3 dH, pH 5–5.5	Peat filtering or addition of peat extract. Fry are very small. Rearing is difficult.
Rivulus *Rivulus agilae*	3 gallons (12 liters)	71.6–80.1°F (22–27°C) 3–8 dH, pH 5.5	♂ very aggressive in too small a tank.
Roloffia chaytori	3 gallons (12 liters)	71.6–75° F (22–24° C) 1–6 dH, pH 6.5–7	No trypaflavine to the eggs, otherwise fry emerge too early and die.

Breeding Instructions for Aquarium Fish

Guppy (*Poecilia reticulata*)
Females 2.4 inches (6 cm), males 1.2 inches (3cm)
Many aquarium-bred forms, distinguished by fin shape and color, are available in pet shops (blue, orange, spotted and so forth).
Origin. Indigenous to southeast South America.
Habitat. Flowing and stagnant water of all kinds, often in coastal areas.
Sexual differences. Males with gonopodium, smaller than females, brilliantly colored; females unprepossessing.
Maintenance tank. Species or community aquarium. (Do not put guppies with elaborate fins together with fin-biting fish.) Size: side length of 16 inches (40 cm) or more. Equipment: not too light, medium-fine tank bed. Spongy side and background foliage, large swimming area. Plants for medium-hard and hard water (for example, *Sagittaria, Vallisneria, Ludwigia,* waterweed, and so on).
Water. Temperature: 73.4 to 78.8°F (23 to 26°C). Hardness: over 10 dH; best between 15 and 30° dH. Very soft water must be hardened (see page 32). pH: 7 to 8.5.
Food. Omnivorous; all kinds of live and dry food, depending on size of fish. Feeding with live food (especially with midge larvae) is conducive to health and successful breeding. Plant food also necessary (as for all live-bearing toothed carp); plant flakes, lettuce leaves, algae in the aquarium.

Reproduction and Rearing
Live-bearing toothed carp also multiply in the community aquarium. However, since the other tank occupants and often even the mothers themselves will eat the newly born, the young must be given the chance to escape. Isolate the pregnant females shortly before birth. Pregnant females have plump, rounded bellies and a gravid spot, a darkened triangular pregnancy mark behind the anal fin at the back of the abdomen through which one can see the ovary. Often the eyes of the young are visible before the birth (see illustrations, page 30). After birth, place the mother back into the maintenance tank.

Breeding tank. Size: side length of 16 inches (40 cm). Equipment: same as for maintenance tank (see above), if possible with a spawning grate (see page 21), through whose openings the young fall after birth so that the mother can't reach them. After birth, remove the grate.
Water. Same as for maintenance tank.
Alternative. You can place the female in a very small aquarium, with a capacity of $2^{1}/_{2}$ to 4 gallons (10 to 15 liters), that is so densely planted with fine-plumed plants that she can move around very slowly. The young can hide in the plant maze, where the mother cannot reach them. The tank must be well ventilated overnight, because the plants use oxygen. After the birth, put the mother in the maintenance tank and transfer the young to the rearing aquarium.
Reproductive behavior. The male courts the female by bending his body into an S shape, approaching her, and darting away. This behavior is repeated over and over. In mating the male extends his gonopodium forward (see illustration, page 46) and approaches the female from below.
Birth. About four to eight weeks after the mating, the female gives birth (up to 150 young). The duration of the pregnancy depends on the maturity of the eggs at the time of mating. If the female has mature eggs that are not fertilized, the eggs are reabsorbed and formed anew. If the female mates during the reabsorption phase, the sperm are stored until the new eggs mature. This prolongs the pregnancy.
Rearing. A few hours after being born, the young eat everything they can manage. Pruebred fry require a well-balanced diet: finely grated dry food; *Artemia, Cyclops,* and *Diaptomus* larvae; algae and other plant food.
Note. Every litter contains a few runts. These are fry that cannot penetrate the water surface in order to fill their swim bladders with air. They never learn to swim properly. You should take them out and prepare them for fodder. If purebred guppies are not maintained under optimal conditions, the offspring form stunted fin appendages.

Silversides
(*Atherinidae*)

These fish inhabit shallow coastal waters in tropical and temperate seas. Some species live part of the time in brackish water and part in fresh water; only a few are pure freshwater dwellers. Species regularly bred in the aquarium are the red-tailed silverside (*Bedotia geayl*) and the Celebes rainbow fish (*Telmatherina ladigesi*).

Red-tailed Silverside
(*Bedotia geayl*), 5.9 inches (15 cm)
Origin. Madagascar.
Habitat. Fast-flowing waters.
Sexual differences. Male bigger, more robustly colored, first dorsal pointed: in the female the first dorsal fin is rounded.
Maintenance tank. Species or community aquarium. Size: side length of 32 inches (80 cm) or more. Equipment: tank bed optional; background and side foliage (mainly fine-plumed types), but also plenty of free swimming space.
Water. 68 to 75°F (20 to 24°C). Hardness: over 10 dH. pH: 7. Change about a quarter to a third of the water weekly, since the fish are susceptible to nitrates, nitrites, bacteria, and infusorians.
Food. Live food of all kinds; the best are insects and insect larvae (black gnat larvae). The fish will feed only at the water surface and ignore any food that sinks to the bottom. Dry food is also possible.

Reproduction and Rearing
The fish spawn near the surface among thick foliage; a few brown eggs are despoited daily. They spawn repeatedly for months. Therefore, it is recommended that the pair be isolated during this period in a breeding tank. Since the adult fish will not attack either the eggs or the fry, the spawn can be left in the breeding tank. The fry develop here until they are returned to the maintenance tank.
Breeding and rearing tank. Size: side length of 28 inches (70 cm) for one pair. Equipment: no tank bed; a few fine-plumed plants or Java moss tufts (anchored with a glass rod).
Water. Temperature: 71.6 to 75.2°F (22 to 24°C).

Hardness: over 10 dH. pH: about 7. Keep the water clean (powerful filtering and water changes as in the maintenance tank).
Reproductive behavior. The male spreads out his fins and leads the bulging female between the plants or over the moss. He then approaches the female from behind, and both fish spawn together. The eggs attach themselves to the plants with long, viscous threads.
Spawn. Contains about 60 eggs.
Emergence of the young. After about six days.
Rearing. First food: paramecia or rotifers; after a week give the fry *Artemia* and *Cyclops* larvae. Powerful aeration and frequent water changes are essential.

Celebes Rainbow Fish
(*Telmatherina ladigesi*), 2.8 inches (7 cm)
Origin. Southeast Asia (Celebes).
Habitat. Smaller rivers and brooks in the highlands.
Sexual differences. Males have more elongated fin rays on the second dorsal and anal fins (the fins become ragged, since the long fin rays are free); the females have shorter fin rays and are paler.
Maintenance tank. Species or community tank. Size: side length of 32 inches (80 cm) or more. Equipment: tank bed of fine sand; dense background and side foliage, but also plenty of room for swimming. Morning sun.
Water. Temperature: 71.6 to 82.4°F (22 to 28°C). Hardness: over 12 dH. pH: 7. The fish do not do well in soft water and will not spawn. Harden very soft tap water or supplement with sea salt (1 to 2 tablespoons of salt to 2½ gallons [10 liters] of water). Change about one-fourth of the water weekly; fish are very susceptible to nitrites, nitrates, bacteria, and infusorians.
Caution. The fish do not tolerate well changes in water hardness.
Food. Live food of all kinds, especially midge larvae and small crustaceans; also food flakes.

Reproduction and Rearing
The fish spawn continuously and eat their eggs. The spawning period lasts several months. It is

Breeding Instructions for Aquarium Fish

Breeding of Popular Live-bearing Toothed Carp

Name	Tank Size	Water Conditions	Comments
Pike-top minnow *Belonesox belizanus* (see illustration page 46)	32 inches (80 cm)	72–79°F (22–26°C) 12–30 dH, pH about 7	Very predatory: species tank 60–80 fry per brood. Feed first with *Cyclops* and *Daphnia*, later with young guppies.
Mosquito fish or Midget live bearer *Heterandria formosa*	16 inches (40 cm)	72–79°F (22–26°C) 15–30 dH, pH 7.5–8.5	No other large fish in tank. Brings forth 1–4 young daily for about 3 weeks. First food for the fry: Mardel's Aquarium Growth Food, paramecia, *euglena*, a little finely grated egg yolk; *Artemia* larvae only after five days.
Black molly *Poecilia sphenops*	32 inches (80 cm)	73.4–82.4°F (23–28°C) 20–35 dH, pH 7.5–8.5	Black variety (black molly) and variety with striped rear fin (liberty molly) available in stores. Seldom found in the wild.
Sailfin molly *Poecilia velifera*	39 inches (100 cm)	77–82.4°F (25–28°C) 25–35 dH, pH 7.5–8.5	Fish from brackish water; plant eaters. 2–3% (or more) sea salt supplement. Adults and fry do not thrive without a vegetarian diet.
Priapella intermedia	24 inches (60 cm)	75.2–78.8°F (24–26°C) 25–35 dH, pH 7–8.5	Somewhat more sensitive than the other species.
Swordtail *Xiphophorus helleri*	39 inches (100 cm)	77–82.4°F (25–28°C) 10–25 dH, pH 7–8.5	Many different varieties (red, black, or spotted) in stores. Seldom found in the wild.
Platy *Xiphophorus maculatus*	24 inches (60 cm)	71.6–78.8°F (22–26°C) 12–30 dH, pH 7–8.5	Many varieties in stores. Seldom found in the wild.
Variegated platy *Xiphophorus variatus*	24 inches (60 cm)	71.6–78.8°F (22–25°C) 12–30 dH, pH 7–8.5	Different varieties in stores. Seldom found in the wild.

therefore necessary to transfer the eggs with the spawning plants to which they are attached into a separate rearing tank on a daily basis.

Breeding suggestion: It is more convenient to have several small aquariums (about 5¼ gallons [20 liters] in volume for a pair, equipped like the breeding tank). After spawning, the parental pair is placed in the next aquarium, and so on.
Breeding tank. Capacity: 13 gallons (50 liters) for several males and females. Equipment: no tank bed; few fine-plumed plants or Java moss tufts (anchored down with a glass rod); floating plants. Disinfect the tanks prior to installation (see page 67); thoroughly disinfect the plants.
Water. Temperature: 71.6 to 75.2°F (22 to 24°C). Hardness: over 12 dH. pH: 7. Filter well.
Reproductive behavior. The male spreads his fins and pursues the female strenuously. The female presses against the plants, the male presses himself against the female, and they spawn together. The eggs adhere to the plants by their viscous threads.
Spawn. Between 20 and 50 eggs in each spawn; less toward the end of the spawning period.
Emergence of the young. After 8 to 11 days.
Rearing. First food: purified paramecia and very fine *Cyclops* larvae; later, *Artemia* larvae.

Breeding suggestion: The fry are more susceptible to infusorians and variations in the water composition than adult fish. Therefore, change the water daily (about one-eighth of the tank) and adjust the hardness and pH if necessary.

Rainbow Fish
(Melanotaeniidae)

Most rainbow fish are maintained and bred under similar conditions. The information below applies to all the species named in the table; exceptions are mentioned.

Rainbow fish
Salmon-red rainbow fish
(*Glossolepis incisus*), 5.9 inches (15 cm)
(see photo, 83)
Boeseman's rainbow fish
(*Melanotaenia boesemani*), female 3.2 inches
(8 cm), male 3.9 inches (10 cm)
(see photo, page 83)
Australian mother-of-pearl rainbow fish
(*Melanotaenia fluviatilis*), 3.9 inches (10 cm)
Dwarf rainbow fish
(*Melanotaenia maccullochi*), 2.8 inches (7 cm)
Great rainbow fish
(*Melanotaenia nigrans*), 2.8 inches (7 cm)
Jewel rainbow fish
(*Melanotaenia trifasciata*), 4.7 inches (12 cm)
Popondetta rainbow fish
(*Popondetta conniae*), 1.9 inches (5 cm)
Honey rainbow fish
(*Pseudomugil mellis*), 1.2 inches (3 cm)

Origin. Australia, New Guinea, and neighboring islands.
Habitat. Running water of all types. The fish are also carried by the overflow into pools and ponds.
Sexual differences. Males are bigger, taller, and more strongly colored than the females.
Maintenance tank. Species or community tank. Size: side length of 19½ inches (50 cm) or more. Equipment: fine tank bed; background and border vegetation of fine-plumed plants; plenty of swimming space. Morning sun. Cover the tank well (the fish leap).
Water. Temperature: 71.6 to 82.4°F (22 to 28°C); for Boeseman's rainbow fish, 80.1 to 86°F (27 to 30°C). Hardness and acidity: between 10 and 20 dH, pH 6 to 6.5. All fish need water low in nitrates. Change water regularly.
Food. Live food, especially insects and insect larvae; also thawed frozen food and dry food of all kinds.

Breeding Instructions for Aquarium Fish

Reproduction and Rearing

All the rainbow fish are continuous spawners. It is possible to breed them in the maintenance tank (species tank), but placing a single pair in a breeding tank is more effective. Most *Melanotaenia* and *Glossolepis* species do not attack the eggs, whereas *Popondetta* and *Pseudomugil* species frequently do. Therefore, remove the parents from the breeding tank after spawning. Or leave the parents in the breeding tank and transfer the plants with the clinging eggs into a special rearing tank.

Breeding tank. Size: side length of 16 inches (40 cm) or more for species up to 1.9 inches (5 cm) in length, 32 inches (80 cm) or more for larger species. Equipment: no tank bed, but fine-plumed plants and Java moss tufts; floating plants are also possible.

Rearing tank. Capacity: 5^1/$_4$ gallons or more. Equipment: no tank bed; spawning plants with eggs; slow filter.

Water. Temperature 75.2 to 86°F (24 to 30°C). Water composition: the same as for the maintenance tank (see above).

Reproductive behavior. The fish are free spawners. The males pursue the females. The partners spawn mostly in the morning between or above the plants. The eggs remain suspended from the plants by their viscous threads.

Spawn. Between 20 and 60 eggs. They are very robust and can be handled. The eggs of the honey rainbow fish can be stored in damp peat like the eggs of many egg-laying toothed carp (see page 96). The development can be followed with the naked eye.

Emergence of the young. After 5 to 11 days, depending on the species.

Rearing. First food: infusorians, rotifers, and ready-made rearing food; after several days, *Artemia* larvae. Change the water in the rearing aquarium regularly.

Glass Perch
(Chandidae)

This family embraces small perch with transparent bodies. The Indian glass perch (*Chanda ranga*) is the most frequently cultivated. It has been imported since 1905. Its rearing was always regarded as very difficult because of the fastidious feeding requirements of the fry.

Indian Glass Perch (*Chanda ranga*),
2.8 inches (7 cm)

Origin. Southeast Asia.

Habitat. Fresh and brackish water.

Sexual differences. The males are more colorful, the swim bladder is pointed, the dorsal and anal fins have blue borders. Females ready to spawn are fatter, the swim bladder is rounded.

Maintenance tank. Species tank. Size: side length of 28 inches or more. Equipment: dark tank bed, since the fish are very nervous; stones and roots for hiding places (males are territorial); dense vegetation (fine-plumed species). Morning sun if possible.

Water. Temperature 68 to 78.8°F (20 to 26°C). Hardness: 10 dH, pH: about 7. Sea salt supplement of 1 to 2 teaspoons per 26 gallons (100 liters) of water, in soft water from 1 to 2 teaspoons per 2^1/$_2$ gallons (10 liters) of water. In hard water the supplement is not absolutely necessary; try it out.

Food. Live food of all kinds, especially insect larvae and small crustaceans; dry food only as a supplement.

Reproduction and Rearing

Well-nourished glass perch often spawn in the maintenance tank, but the fry cannot be reared there (see below) even though the parents do not attack the eggs. At spawning time place a pair of fish into the breeding tank; after spawning, put them back again into the maintenance tank or into a wider breeding tank (they spawn for several days at most). The fry are raised in the breeding tank.

Breeding Instructions for Aquarium Fish

Breeding tank. Capacity: 4 to 8 gallons (15 to 30 liters) for one pair. Equipment: black-striped tank bed or a thin layer of sand; roots as hiding places; fine-plumed plants that tolerate hard water (for example, chickweed) or floating fern (*Ceratopteris*).
Water. Temperature: 75.2 to 82.4°F (24 to 28°C). Hardness: 10 dH. pH: about 7. Sea salt supplement if necessary (see above).

Breeding suggestion: Adding fresh water and raising the temperature promote spawning, especially if both partners are separated and fed well before spawning.
Reproductive behavior. The fish spawn mostly in the morning. The male extends his fins, swims around the female, and prods her with his mouth. The fish spawn between the plants. The eggs cling to the plants.
Spawn. Up to 200 eggs. To prevent fungal growth, add trypaflavine (1 gram per 26 gallons [100 liters] of water).
Emergence of the young. After 18 to 24 hours; the fry swim freely on the following day.
Rearing. First food: freshly hatched *Diaptomus* and *Cyclops*. In feeding *Cyclops*, give only as much as can be eaten in one hour (so that the larvae will not develop into adult *Cyclops* and attack the fry). This means that you must feed every hour. Since the fry do not hunt for food, darken the tank with paper and let light shine on only a small area. The fry and their prey will be drawn there, and the fry can eat easily.

Breeding suggestion: It is pointless to breed glass perch if you don't have a steady supply of *Diaptomus*. Glass perch fry also eat large rotifers if need be, but the rearing results are not as good.

Blue Perch
(Badidae)

The family of blue perch embraces a single species, the Indian blue perch (*Badis badis*), which is reared regularly in the aquarium.

Indian blue perch (*Badis badis*), 3.2 inches (8 cm)
Origin. India.
Habitat. Stagnant water.
Sexual differences. Male is more colorful, with concave ventral line; female ventral ilne is convex.
Maintenance tank. Species tank. Size: side length of 24 inches or more. Equipment: tank bed of fine gravel or coarse sand, not too light; hiding places and caves of stones, roots, coconut shells, and flowerpots; vegetation appropriate for the water conditions; light cover of floating plants.
Water. Temperature: 73.4 to 78.8°F (23 to 26°C). Hardness: relatively unimportant, mostly between 8 and 12 dH. pH: about 7.
Food. Live food of all kinds, appropriate for the size of the fish; dry food is often accepted.

Reproduction and Rearing
The fish spawn regularly in the species tank. With small tanks, take the females out after spawning and shelter them in a special aquarium.
Alternative: Place the pair in the breeding tank. After spawning, return the female to the maintenance tank, otherwise she will be pursued by the male. The male guard the spawn and keeps the young together until the yolk sac is consumed. After the young swim on their own, return the male to the maintenance tank.
Breeding tank. Size: side length of 20 inches (50 cm) or more. Equipment: same as for the maintenance tank (see above).
Water. Temperature: 78.8 to 86°F (26 to 30°C). Hardness: 8 to 12 dH. pH: about 7. Water composition is of minor importance.
Reproductive behavior. Spawning usually takes place in a cave.
Spawn. Between 30 and 100 eggs.
Emergence of the young. After three days; two days later the fry swim on their own.
Rearing. First food: *Artemia* larvae (also other larvae); later finely-grated pond food of proper size (see page 61).

Breeding suggestion: In larger, adequately covered species tanks (about 39 inches [100 cm] side length), two to three males and four to six females can be kept. The females, after spawning, hide among stones and plants and need not be taken out. The young are scarcely bothered by the adult fish. During the first days of swimming on their own, they feed on the microorganisms in the aquarium; three to four days after swimming on their own, the feeding begins: small amounts of *Artemia* larvae, rotifers, or finely sifted pond food two to three times daily. The young perch among the little stones of the tank bed and catch whatever floats past them.

Cichlids
(Cichlidae)

Of the some 160 cichlid genera with over 900 species, about 700 species live in Africa, over 200 in America, and three in India. Cichlids have adapted to the most varied ecological conditions. Many live in rapids, others in river water close to the ocean, and some even in alkaline lakes with a pH of 10.5 in which other fish would not survive.

Forms of Brood Care

In adapting to different environmental conditions, the cichlids have developed very dissimilar reproductive strategies, which can be divided into three main categories: open breeders, hidden (cave) breeders, and mouthbreeders. Between these groups there exist transitions.

Open breeders
Open breeders spawn on stones or on plants. Usually the spawn is very large and can include several thousand eggs. The small, oval eggs are camouflaged or transparent and cling to the substratum (that is, stones, plants, roots, or aquarium panes); some have short stalks. Sexual differences between males and females are not very profound; often, however, the males are larger and have longer, more pointed dorsal and anal fins. In many species the males develop a fat-storage hump on their foreheads, the size of

which—at least in *Cichlassoma (Amphilopus) citrinellum*—depends on the rank of the male and on the presence of rivals. The hump can increase or decrease in size in a matter of hours. Male and female discus fish (*Symphysonon*) and angelfish (*Pterophyllum*) can be differentiated before spawning by the shape of their genital papilla (the male's is pointed; the female's is blunt).

The fish pair for breeding and may remain together even after the spawning period. Often, however, the males wander off and start a new brood with another female that is ready to spawn. If several females are present and accessible (under favorable rearing conditions), open-breeding males may become polygamous.

Hidden (cave) breeders
Hidden breeders lay bigger and more colorful eggs than the open breeders; however, the spawn is smaller (less than 200 eggs). The males of most hidden breeders are much bigger and often more strikingly colored than the females.

Cave breeders attach their eggs to the roof of the cave (see photo, page 19). After hatching, the fry hang down the cave roof.

Mouth breeders
Mouthbreeding cichlids can be differentiated into ovophiles (from the Latin *ovum*, or egg, and the Greek *philos*, or friend) and larvophiles. *Ovophile mouthbreeders* (see photo on the inside front cover) take the eggs into their mouths right after spawning. The best known ovophile mouth-breeders come from the East African lakes (Lake Tanganyika and Lake Malawi). They form pairs only during spawning; frequently the females wander from male to male.

Males of many species have developed egg decoys (structures that resemble the eggs of the respective species). Best known among these are the egg spots on the anal fin of the *Haplochromis* males and their relatives, species of the genera *Pseudotropheus, Labetropheus, Melanochromis,* and *Aulonocara*. The egg decoys attract the female to the genital opening of the male, from which she sucks in sperm to fertilize the eggs in her mouth (see illustration, page 50). This guarantees that the eggs of the female are fertilized by the sperm of the territorial owner rather than by those of the satellite males, who, disguised as females, deposit their sperm in the spawning pits of the territorial male. (see page 50).

Other egg decoys have also developed. The males of *Oreochromis macrochir* and other *Oreochromis* species possess little grapelike appendages on their genital papilla that resemble the egg bundles of the females. The males of the *Ophthalmochromis* species have sharply elongated ventral fins with rounded, yolk-colored ends, which they proffer to the females while spawning. The function is the same as with the egg spots: the female tries to gather the so-called eggs and, in the process, sucks in sperm from the genital papilla of the male. The males of these highly specialized mouthbreeders are mostly larger and more splendidly colored than the females. The spawn consists of fewer than 70 eggs (30 to 40 eggs in many species). *Tropheus* species lay only 10 to 15 eggs. The eggs are big, rich in yolk, and colored a brilliant yellow-orange. *Larvophile mouthbreeders,* like open breeders, spawn on stones (see photo, page 55). However, when the larvae emerge (after several days), they take the larvae into their mouths and tend them until the yolk sacs are consumed. After that they handle the brood just like other cichlid parents. The best known larvophile mouthbreeders are a few species of the South American genus *Geophagus* (see photos on page 56 and back cover) and the West African genus *Chromidotilapia*.

Rearing and Family Structures

In addition to the various reproductive strategies, different family structures are observed among cichlid species, depending on the roles of the males and females in territorial protection and the care of the eggs and young.

Parental families. Males and females share equally in the tasks of territorial protection, cleaning the spawning bed, fanning the eggs, caring for the larvae, and guiding and protecting the fry. The parents remain together until the fry are independent (although the males stray occasionally). External sexual differences are not prominent.

Father–mother family. The sexual partners enter into a mating union as in a parental family. Both share equally in defending the territory and cleaning the spawning bed. But they divide their tasks in caring for the eggs and larvae. The female is the primary caretaker, while the male concerns himself mostly with the territory. The fry are guided by both parents. The sexes are easy to distinguish by body form and color.

Harem-forming (polygamous) family. The roles of the sexes are still further differentiated. The female alone undertakes the care of the eggs and the young. The male concerns himself exclusively with the defense of the territory. This family structure is found in all cave-breeding, harem-forming cichlids. A large male gains a territory by fighting. A number of females settle in the territory, depending on the number of favorable spawning places, and pair off with the male. The male is therefore polygamous; the females are monogamous and are often aggressive toward each other. The females defend their individual spawning caves from predators. The young live in the territory of the parents, and are thereby well protected against predators.

Mother family. Here the female alone takes over the care of the eggs and young without staying in the territory of the male. The sexual partners come together only for spawning; the female can change partners during spawning. The sexes usually differ very sharply in size and color; however, they can also be almost identical, and are capable of imitating the behavior of the other sex.

Father family. In this family only the male concerns himself with the eggs and brood after spawning. The female is territorial, aggressive, and mates with the male. The fish form a pair, select a spawning place, and the male fertilizes the eggs that the female lays there. The male then takes the eggs into his mouth and carries them around for about two weeks until the young are capable of taking care of themselves. The number of eggs that the male takes into his mouth depends on the size of the male and the aggressiveness of the female. If the male is relatively large and the female is not very aggressive, the female also takes some eggs into her mouth. If the female is much stronger than the male, only the male takes the eggs and tends them alone.

Special Features of a Cichlid Aquarium

Cichlids are best kept and bred in large species aquariums (if necessary also in the company of other, equally large and powerful fish with different requirements).

Tank Size
Male cichlids, especially during the spawning period, are territorial and very aggressive toward all fish, in particular males of the same species. If the tank is too small, males can fight to the death over territory or females. Females, too, can be killed if they are not ready to spawn and have no opportunity to withdraw from the male's territory. In small tanks cichlids are frequently aggressive at all times. They establish ranking order in which the strongest (usually the largest) male dominates all the other fish, the second largest chases all those smaller than himself, and so on. The smallest fish may be chased to exhaustion and death. In the tables pertaining to the cichlids, the smallest size of the aquarium for sexually mature but not yet fully grown fish is given under the heading "Species Tank." It is better if the tank is bigger; the more spacious a cichlid aquarium, the more tranquil are the inhabitants.

Equipment
Many cichlids chew through the upper tank bed layer in search for something edible; therefore, the tank bed should not be too tough.
Cichlid aquariums must be divided by separators of stones or twigs to enable the subordinate fish to escape from the dominant fish. Stone structures should stand directly on the tank floor so that they will not be undermined and collapse. Some should reach to the water surface, since the weakest fish are always chased to the top. This is especially important for the maintenance of East African mouthbreeding cichlids.
Cave breeders need shelters made of stones, earthenware pipes, coconut shells, and flowerpots. Cichlids from tropical rain forests (for example, fish of the genus *Pelvicachromis*, discus fish, and angelfish) need twigs. You can forego foliage with many species. When large fish dig spawning pits, plants are uprooted or bitten off. You can use large, robust plants as territorial boundaries and, if necessary, place them in flower pots covered with big stones. Many cichlids eat plants, for example, many mouthbreeders from Lake Malawi and Lake Tanganyika, which in the wild eat algae from the rocks. For cichlids from tropical rain forest waters floating plants are indispensable. In bright light many species become nervous, which can lead to dangerous fights between members of the species (See also tables on pages 116-117).

1. Example of an Open Breeder

Blue Acara (*Aequidens pulcher*),
up to 8 inches (20 cm).
Origin. Northern South America.
Habitat. Calm waters with many hiding places.
Sexual differences. Dorsal and anal fins in male often more extended than in the female.
Maintenance tank. Species tank for a pair (see above). Size: side length of 32 inches (80 cm) or more. Equipment: tank bed of coarse sand and fine gravel; stones and roots as hiding places; hardy plants (*Sagittaria, Vallisneria, Echinodorus,* sword plants).
Water. Temperature: 64.4 to 77°F (18 to 25°C). Hardness: 7 to 15 dH, if necessary to 25 dH. pH: 6.5 to 8. Frequent water changes (a third of the tank once or twice a week), otherwise the fish are susceptible to disease.
Food. Mainly live food (insects, insect larvae, clean rainworms, fish meat), but also dry food (food flakes, food pellets, and even trout pellets for large fish).

Breeding Instructions for Aquarium Fish

Reproduction and Rearing
Breeding takes place in the maintenance tank.
Remove the fry from the tank when the parents no longer care for the brood (about six weeks after emergence).
Breeding tank. Not necessary.
Water. Increase temperature to 78.8 to 82.4°F (26 to 28°C).
Reproductive behavior. Open breeders with parental family. Calm, aggressive only before spawning and during brood tending. Both partners defend the territory and clean the spawning bed (horizontal or diagonal stones). During spawning the female lays a few eggs and the male fertilizes them. Then the female lays more eggs, and so on. After spawning the partners share in caring for the brood. They guard the spawn, fan it, and keep it clean. They assist the young during hatching by sucking them out of the eggshells. Both parents guide the fry and defend them fiercely.
Spawn. Several hundred eggs.
Emergence of the young. At 77 to 84.2°F (25 to 28°C), on the fourth day. The parents spit the larvae into small cone-shaped holes, where they remain for five days; after five days they swim on their own.
Rearing. First food: *Artemia* larvae, later *Cyclops* larvae and tiny worms, then other live foods of appropriate size.

Breeding suggestion: Open breeders almost always form parental or father-mother families. If the parental fish are very aggressive toward each other, place some surface fish (for example, zebra and barbs) into the tank. These will be perceived by the cichlids as a threat to their young and will draw the couple closer together.

2. Example of an Open Breeder

Angelfish (*Pterophyllum scalare*) 5.9 inches (15 cm)
(See photo, page 20, and illustration, page 65).
Origin. Tropical South America.
Habitat. Calm and protected coastal regions with roots, trees, and plants.

Sexual differences. Genital papilla is pointed in the male, round in the female (see page 111).
Maintenance tank. Species or community aquarium (see page 113). Size: side length of 32 inches (80 cm) or more. Equipment: fine tank bed; twigs and dense border foliage of large-leaved plants (mainly *Echinodorus* species).
Water. Temperature: 75.2 to 78.8°F (24 to 26°C). Hardness: 7 to 17 dH, even harder at low carbonate levels. pH: 6.7 to 7.5. Regular water changes (one-fourth of the tank every 3 weeks).
Food. Live and dry food; small portions of midge larvae (the fish overeat).

Reproduction and Rearing
Breeding takes place in the maintenance tank.
When the pair starts to mate, remove the other tank occupants. Take the fry out of the tank when the parents no longer care for them.
Breeding tank. Not necessary.
Water. Temperature: raise to 78.8 to 82.4°F (26 to 28°C). Hardness: 4 to 6 dH. pH: 6.5.
Reproductive behavior. Open breeders with parental family. The fish are peaceful, do not damage plants. The breeding partners clean hard plant leaves (*Echinodorus* or giant *Vallisneria*), frequently even stones or the heater. They spawn like other open breeders (see page 111). Both partners clean, fan, and defend the spawn until the larvae hatch. The parents help the young to hatch by sucking them out of the eggshells. They attach the larvae to leaves, stones, or aquarium panes, to which they adhere by the hooks on their heads. When they fall off, they are scooped up and reattached. When the fry are free-swimming, they are guided by both parents.
Spawn. Up to 1,000 eggs.
Emergence of the young. At 78.8 to 86°F (26 to 30°C), after 24 to 36 hours; fry are free-swimming four to five days after emergence.
Rearing. First food: *Artemia* larvae, rotifers, *Cyclops* larvae, later also eelworms.

Breeding Instructions for Aquarium Fish

3. Example of an Open Breeder

Green Discus

(**Symphysodon aequifasciatus**) 7.1 inches (18 cm)
(See photo on inside front cover and illustration on page 49).
Origin. South America, central Amazon and tributaries.
Habitat. Calm coastal regions of tropical forest rivers with tree roots and fallen branches.
Sexual differences. Genital papilla pointed in the male, round in the female (see page 111).
Maintenance tank. Species tank. Size: side length of 47 inches (120 cm) or more. Equipment: dark, soft tank bed, light foliage (for example, *Cryptocoryne*); subdued light or loose floating plant cover (for example, *Ceratopteris thalictroides*); twigs and larger, lime-free stones. Iron-containing plant fertilizer is desirable. (In the wild discus fish live in water with a high iron content. Iron deficiency makes the fish pale and susceptible to disease.)
Water. Water level over 20 inches (50 cm). Temperature: 78.8 to 82.4°F (26 to 28°C). Hardness: 2 to 3 dH. pH: 6.5. Regular water changes (a tenth of the tank daily or a fourth every three weeks).
Food. Live food (midge larvae, water fleas, other water insects, rainworms, prawn krill, some *Tubiflex*), some fish meat, high quality dry food.

My suggestion: Don't keep angelfish together with discus fish, they can infect susceptible discus fish with *Hexamita*.

Reproduction and Rearing
Breeding in a maintenance tank is possible. Separate the fry from the parents at least 10 days after they are free-swimming. Alternatively put a pair of fish into a breeding tank.
Breeding tank. Size: 28 x 28 x 28 inches (70 x 70 x 70 cm). Equipment: No tank bed, plants, two stone disks and a spawning cone or an unpainted clay vase in order to keep the water as clean as possible.
Water. Temperature: 82.4 to 87.8° F (28 to 31° C). Hardness: 1 to 3 dH, CH (carbonate hardness): 0.5 to 1.5 degrees. pH: 5 to 6.2.

Reproductive behavior. Open breeders with parental family. Quiet, do not damage plants. Mating and spawning the same as with angelfish (see page 114). The fish spawn on carefully cleaned plant leaves or stones. Care of eggs, help in emergence, care of larvae are the same as with angelfish.
Spawn. Up to 250 eggs.
Emergence of the young. At 82.4 to 86°F (28 to 30°C), on the third day; the fry are free-swimming six days after emergence.
Rearing. After they become free-swimming, the fry eat a food that is secreted from the skin of the parents, (mainly on the back and sides). This food may also contain protozoa and small algae. The fry must be fed by their parents for at least 10 days, since the secreted food cannot be replaced by artificial rearing means. From the fifth day the parental secretion can be supplemented by *Artemia* larvae and later by *Cyclops* larvae, eel worms, and tiny pond food (see page 61).

Breeding suggestion: Once the fry are free-swimming, the water hardness in the rearing tank should be raised very gradually, so that the fish adjust to the local water conditions. If possible, change one-fourth of the water in the rearing tank every day, and add some tap water to the fresh water. The breeding of discus fish succeeds only if the high demands of temperature, water composition, and food are satisfied. Discus fish are extremely susceptible to disease if they are not kept under optimal conditions.
Note. There are two species of discus fish and several subspecies, all of which are bred in the same manner.

Example of a Cave Breeder

Agassizi Dwarf Cichlid

(**Apistogramma agassizi**) 3.2 inches (8 cm)
Origin. South America, in the southern Amazon.
Habitat. Smaller waters rich in hiding places.

Breeding Data for Popular Cichlids: Open Breeders

Name	Species Tank	Water Conditions	Comments ♂ = male, ♀ = female
Anomalochromis thomasi	28 inches (70 cm)	78.8–80.1°F (26–27°C) 6–16 dH, pH 6.5–7	Parental family. Not very aggressive. Spawn on plants or stones.
Oscar, velvet cichlid *Astronotus ocellatus*	79 inches (200 cm)	78.8–86°F (26–30°C) 3–20 dH, pH 6–7	Parental family. Aggressive in small aquariums. Spawn on stones. Regular partial water change.
Cichlasoma (Amphilophus) citrinellum	59 inches (150 cm)	75.2–82.4°F (24–28°C) 10–25 dH, pH 6.5–7.5	Parental family. Aggressive. Spawn on stones or other foundations. Parents form skin slime as food for the young. Orange-yellow, whitish and gray specimens.
Cichlasoma (Theraps) maculicauda	47 inches (120 cm)	73.4–82.4°F (23–28°C) 10–25 dH, pH about 7	Parental family. Aggressive. Eat plants. Spawn on stones.
Convict cichlid *Cichlasoma (Archocentrus) nigrofasciatum*	32 inches (80 cm)	75.2–80.1°F (24–27°C) 10–25 dH, pH about 7	Father–mother family. Aggressive. Spawn often in caves or on protected stones under roots and so on (transition to cave breeders).
Cichlasoma (Parapetenia) salvini	32 inches (80 cm)	75.2–86°F (24–30°C) 10–25 dH, pH 6.5–7	Parental family. Aggressive. Spawn on stones.
Checkerboard cichlid *Crenicara fillamentosa*	24 inches (60 cm)	78.8–80°F (26–27°C) 0.1–2 dH pH about 5.5 or lower	Harem-forming family. Nervous (add characins or other gentle fish). Spawn on leaves or stones. Very clean water (eye fungus develops in dirty or too hard water).
Crenicara punctulata	32 inches (80 cm)	78.8–80.1°F (26–27°C) about 10 dH, pH 6–7	Harem-forming family. Sex transformation.
Orange chromide *Etroplus maculatus*	24 inches (60 cm)	77–82.4°F (25–28°C) 3–10 dH, pH 7. Sea salt addition: 1–2 teaspoons to 2½ gallons (10 liters)	Parental family. Spawn on stones or roots. Parents produce skin secretion as food for fry. In fresh water often fungus diseases.
Jewel cichlid *Hemichromis bimaculatus*	39 inches (100 cm)	73.4–82.4°F (23–26°C) 4–16 dH, pH about 7	Parental family. Slightly aggressive. Spawn on stones. Other *Hemichromis* species have equal requirements.
Heros severus	39 inches (100 cm)	77–82°F (25–29°C) about 5 dH, pH 6–6.5	Parental family. Slightly aggressive. Spawn on stones. Maintenance like discus fish, although not as fastidious.

Breeding Instructions for Aquarium Fish

Rainbow cichlid *Herotilapia multispinosa*	28 inches (70 cm)	77–80.1°F (25–27°C) 5–10 dH, pH about 7	Parental family. Slightly aggressive. Spawn on stones or other foundations. Tendency to hidden care.
Laetacara curviceps	24 inches (60 cm)	78.8–84.2°F (26–29°C) to 14 dH, pH 6–6.8	Parental family. Slightly aggressive. Spawn on stones or roots. Regular partial water change, otherwise susceptible to disease.
Mesonauta festiva	39 inches (100 cm)	77–82.4°F (25–28°C) 6–16 dH, pH 6.5–7	Parental family. Slightly aggressive, nervous. Spawn on plant leaves or stones.
Papiliochromis altispinosa	24 inches (60 cm)	77–82.4°F, (25–28°C) 3–16 dH, pH about 7	Parental family. Hardly aggressive. Less susceptible to chemicals than *Papiliochromis ramirezi*. Occasionally takes larvae into mouth.
Papiliochromis ramirezi	20 inches (50 cm)	80.1–84.2°F, (27–29°C) 3–8 dH, pH about 7. Peat filtering or peat extract.	Parental family. Hardly aggressive. Spawn on stones or in caves. Very sensitive to chemicals of all kinds. With partial water change always add water conditioners.
Thorichthys meeki	32 inches (80 cm)	25.2–80.1°F, (24–27°C) 10–25 dH, pH about 7	Parental family. Slightly aggressive. Spawn on stones.
Tiliapia joka	39 inches (100 cm)	77–80°F, (25–27°C) 1–12 dH, pH 6.5–7	Father–mother family. Relatively peaceful. Strong tendency to hidden breeding.
Tilapia mariae	39 inches (100 cm)	75.2–82.4°F, (24–28°C) 6–25 dH, pH about 7	Parental family. Aggressive toward members of own species. Tendency toward hidden breeding.
Triangle cichlid	47 inches (120 cm)	80.1–87.8°F, (27–31°C) 2–5 dH, pH about 6	Parental family. Spawn on plants or stones, mostly in shade. Parents form skin secretion as food for fry. Peat filter. Maintenance same as for discus fish.

Breeding Instructions for Aquarium Fish

Sexual differences. Males are substantially larger and more colorful than females, their dorsal, anal, and tail fins are much longer.

Maintenance tank. Species tank. As with many other harem-forming cave breeders, it is best to keep several females with one large male. Size: side length of 32 inches (80 cm) or more. Equipment: fine, dark tank bed; caves and hiding places between stones and twigs. Flower pots, coconut shells, or clay pipes half sunk into the tank bed as breeding caves. Cover the cave entrance with stones and leave small holes through which only the females can enter. Dense foliage; also fine-plummed species.

Water. Temperature: 71.6 to 75.2°F (22 to 24°C). Hardness 8 to 10 dH. pH: 6 to 6.5. Good filtering, regular water changes. The fish are susceptible to nitrites, nitrates, heavy metals, various chemicals, and lack of oxygen.

Food. Mainly live food, suitable for the size of the fish.

Reproduction and Rearing

Leave the male and females in the maintenance tank. The fry are taken out and transferred to a rearing tank as soon as the mother stops caring for them.

Breeding tank. Not necessary.

Water. Raise the temperature to 77 to 82.4°F (25 to 28°C). Lower the water hardness to 4 to 8 dH. pH: 6 to 6.5.

Reproductive behavior. Harem-forming cave breeders. A large male owns a territory and mates with several females, which defend their mating territory against each other. A female ready to spawn swims to the male. He follows the female into the breeding cave, she crawls inside and lays her eggs on the previously cleaned cave roof, and the male fertilizes the eggs. If the entrance is too narrow for the male, he emits sperm outside and propels them with his tail and fins flappings into the cave. When the female has deposited all her eggs, she drives the male and all the other fish from the vicinity of the cave and cleans and fans the spawn until the larvae emerge. The male defends only the outer perimeter. When the larvae emerge, the mother chews them out of the eggshell,

lifts them up to the cave roof, or places them in a hole on the floor of the cave. The female alone guides the young. If other females in the male's territory have young, the fry always follow the female that is next to them, so that fry of different ages can mix together.

Spawn. Includes 50 to 100 eggs.

Emergence of the young. At 78.8 to 82.4° F (26 to 28° C), after three days; six to eight days after emergence, the female guides the fry.

Rearing. The mother guides the fry to stones, wood or plants that are overgrown with algae and microorganisms. Therefore, it is not necessary to feed the fry during the first two to three days. After that you should start feeding the fry with *Artemia* larvae.

Example of an Ovophile Mouth Breeder

Melanochromis auratus 4.7 inches (12 cm)

Origin. East Africa (Lake Malawi)

Habitat. Rocky shores.

Sexual differences. Male is striped black–turquoise. Female is somewhat smaller and striped black–golden yellow; in contrast to the male, she has no egg spots.

Maintenance tank. Species tank or community aquarium with similar cichlids. Size: side length of 39 inches (100 cm) or more. Equipment: Large stone structures with many hiding places at the back wall; broader stone structures (that reach to the water surface if possible) as territorial dividers in the central area. A few hardy plants can be put in.

Water. Temperature: about 78.8°F (26°C). Hardness: 10 to 15 dH (or higher). pH: 7 to 8.

Food. Live and dry food.

Barbs during mating.

In most *Barbus* species the actual spawning is very fast. Here is a phase in the mating of the dotted barb (*Barbus ticto*). The more colorful male chases the female through the tank. For spawning the couple seeks fine-plumed plants (here a *Myriophylum* species). The eggs cling firmly to the plants and are not taken care of by the parents.

Breeding Instructions for Aquarium Fish

Reproduction and Rearing

Keep one male with five to eight females together in the maintenance tank. The female keeps the fertilized eggs in her mouth until the emergence of the young (about three weeks). Remove the female about 14 days after spawning, and isolate her in a rearing tank with a side length of about 20 inches (50 cm), equipped like the maintenance tank.

Breeding tank. Not necessary.

Water. Same as for the maintenance tank (see above).

Reproductive behavior. Ovophile mouthbreeders with mother family. No pair bonding. The male repeatedly swims toward the female and, with various body movements, tries to entice her to the spawning pit. If a female is ready to spawn, she follows him, lies on her side in the spawning pit, and releases one or more eggs. She turns around immediately and takes them into her mouth. Thereupon the male again lies on his side with outspread anal fins, and the female tries to gather up the egg decoys from the male's anal fin. She thus sucks sperm into her mouth. Once the female has deposited all her eggs, she leaves the spawning pit with the spawn and retreats to a protected place. While she is tending the brood in her mouth (about three weeks), the female doesn't eat or eats very little.

Spawn. About 30 to 50 eggs, sometimes more.

Emergence of the young. After about three weeks the fry are let out of the mother's mouth. By then they are already well developed, and have a very small yolk sac or none at all.

Rearing. First food: *Artemia* larvae, finely sifted water flea, finely grated dry food (for example, Tetra-Ovin).

Breeding suggestion: Do not remove females from the tank immediately after spawning; they often spit out the eggs or swallow them. Isolate them in rearing tanks only after about 14 days. Females kept alone release the young from their mouths much earlier than females in a community aquarium. *Simochromis* and *Tropheus* females can hold the fry in their mouths for a month without the latter going hungry, because of the large food reserves in the yolk sacs. When kept alone, however, *Simochromis* females spit out their young after the seventh or ninth day, bore a hole in the tank bed, and there tend them further, like open breeders. Only when danger threatens do they take the fry into their mouths. Females who hold the fry in their mouths for weeks get very thin and need a long time until they are again ready to spawn.

Example of a Larvophile Mouthbreeder

Paraguay Mouthbreeder
(***Gymnogeophagus balzanii***) 7.9 inches (20 cm)

Origin. South America, Paraguay.

Habitat. Calm waters rich in hiding places.

Sexual differences. Males have longer, extended, fins; older males with large hump on the forehead. In females the rear part of the gill covering is orange-red.

Maintenance tank. Species tank with one fish pair. Size: side length of 39 inches (100 cm) or more. Equipment: tank bed of fine sand; hiding places, caves of stones or roots, hardy plants in pots on territorial boundaries.

Water. Temperature: 71.6 to 78.8°F (22 to 26°C). Hardness: 8 to 13 dH. pH: about 7.

Food. Live and dry food of all kinds.

Many school fish, like the zebra fish (*Brachydanio rerio*) shown here, also spawn in a school. The spawning happens so quickly that the human eye is often unable to observe it. The fish speed past each other and emit eggs and sperm. In the photo this takes place during a fraction of a second.

121

Breeding Instructions for Aquarium Fish

Breeding Data of Popular Cichlids: Cave Breeders

Name	Species Tank	Water Conditions	Comments ♂ = male, ♀ = female
Dwarf cichlid *Apistogramma borellii*	24 inches (60 cm)	77–82.4°F (25–28°C) 3–8 dH, pH 6–6.5	Harem-forming family. Slightly aggressive. Spawn on cave roof. Susceptible to water pollution and chemicals.
Julidochromis marlieri	32 inches (80 cm)	75.2–80.1°F (24–27°C) 12–20 dH, pH 7.5–8.5	Parental family, with tendency to father–mother family. Slightly aggressive. ♂ polygamous. If possible spawn on cave roof. Fry live for months in parental territory.
Lamprologus ocellatus	20 inches (50 cm)	77–80.1°F (25–27°C) 12–20 dH, pH 7.5–8.5	Harem-forming or mother family. Slightly aggressive. The ♂ bury empty snail shells in the sand, which they defend as spawning caves.
Lamprologus brichardi	24 inches (60 cm)	77–82.4°F (25–28°C) 12–20 dH, pH 7.5–8.5	Parental family with tendency toward harem-forming family. Slightly aggressive. Spawn on cave roof. Fry live for months in the territory of the parents, share in the care of younger siblings.
Golden-eyed dwarf cichlid *Nannacara anomala*	28 inches (70 cm)	77–86°F (25–30°C) 8–12 dH, pH 6.2–6.8	Father–mother family, in small aquariums mother family, since the ♂ attacks the ♀ violently; take out the ♀. Aggressive. Spawn on cave wall or roof or submerged stones.
Emperor cichlid *Pelvidhrommis pulcher* see photo, page 19	24 inches (60 cm)	77–82.4°F, (25–28°C) 8–12 dH, pH 6.5	Father–mother family. Aggressive. Spawn mostly on cave roof.
Lion-headed cichlid *Steatocranus casuarius*	32 inches (80 cm)	78.8–84.2°F (26–29°C) 8–17 dH, pH 6.5–7.5	Father–mother family. Aggressive. Monogamous. Inhabitants of rapids, (therefore, create a current in the tank).
Brichard's African dward cichlid *Teleogramma*	32 inches (80 cm)	73.4–78.8°F (23–26°C) 1–10 dH, pH 6.5–7.5	Harem-forming family. Aggressive. Spawn on cave wall or roof. Inhabitants of rapids (create a current in the tank).

Breeding Instructions for Aquarium Fish

Breeding Data of Popular Cichlids: Ovophile Mouth Breeders

Genera exclusively found in Lake Malawi
(Egg decoys and fertilization by the "egg-spot method")
Water conditions: 77–82.4°F (25–28°C), 10–15 dH or higher, pH 7.5–8.5 (to 9 possible).

Name	Species Tank	Comments ♂ = male, ♀ = female
Aulonocara jacobfreibergi	39 inches (100 cm)	Mother family. Relatively shy. Egg spots on anal fin of the ♂, sometimes also on ♀.
Labidochromis vellicans	39 inches (100 cm)	Mother family. Slightly aggressive. Picks small crustaceans and other small organisms from plant growth with its pointed snout.
"Haplochromis" boadzulu	39 inches (100 cm)	Mother family. Aggressive. Egg spots in ♂, often even in ♀.
Zebra Malawi Cichlid *Pseudotropheus Zebra*	39 inches (100 cm)	Mother family. Aggressive. Eggs spots. Within the species there are different form and color types. Similar in caring and breeding to *Laebeotropheus* species.

Genera found exclusively in Lake Tanganyika
(Egg decoys and fertilization by the "egg-spot method")
Water conditions: 77–82.4°F (25–28°C), 12–18 dH or more, pH 7.5–8.5 (to 9 possible).

Name	Species Tank	Comments ♂ = male, ♀ = female
Tanganyika clown *Eretmodus cyanosticus*	32 inches (80 cm)	Parental family. Slightly aggressive. Monogamous. Fertilization by egg-spot method, but no egg decoys on anal fins. ♀ takes eggs in mouth. After about a week, she gives the eggs/larvae to the ♂, who tends them in his mouth for another week. Both guide the young fry. Good ventilation and filtering; very clean water; frequent partial water changes (to ¹/₃ of the tank per week).
Petrochromis trewavasae	47 inches (120 cm)	Mother family. Aggressive. Fertilization by egg-spot method. Egg spots can be missing.
Blunt-headed Cichlid *Tropheus moorei*	47 inches (120 cm)	Mother family. Aggressive. Egg spots are lacking. Plant and algae eater. Provide plant food. Many color forms.
Yellow Sand Cichlids *Xenotilapia flavipinnis*	39 inches (100 cm)	Parental family. After spawning, ♂ takes eggs into his mouth and after about a week he gives them to the ♀. Both parents guard free-swimming fry. Species cannot mix in with other cichlids.

Breeding Instructions for Aquarium Fish

Other Ovophile Mouthbreeders Name	Species Tank	Water Conditions	Comments ♂ = male, ♀ = female
Burton's Mouthbreeder *Astatotilapia burtoni*	39 inches (100 cm)	78.8-82.4°F (26-28°C) 10-18 dH, pH 7-8.5	Mother family. Aggressive. Egg spots. ♂ live in colonies, build spawning pits, and mate with ♀ swimming past.
Chromidotilapia finleyi	39 inches (100 cm)	75.2-82.4°F (24-28°C) 1-7 dH, pH 5-7	Parental family. Aggressive. Spawn on stones, wood or big leaves. After spawning, ♀ takes eggs in mouth, defends territory. Partners exchange eggs and tasks daily until fry are free-swimming. Differences in breeding behavior between various color forms
Chromidotilapia guentheri	39 inches (100 cm)	77-82.4°F (25-28°C) 5-10 dH, pH about 7	Parental family/father-mother family. Aggressive. Spawn on stones or other foundations. After spawning ♂ takes eggs into mouth. Both parents take care of free-swimming fry. ♀ also takes fry into her mouth when danger threatens.
"Geophagus" steindachneri see photo page 56	47 inches (120 cm)	78.8-84.2°F (26-29°C) 5-15 dH, pH 6.5-7	Mother family. Aggressive. ♂ with yellow spots on corner of mouth. Apparently works similarly to egg spots. Spawn on stones. ♀ takes eggs into mouth after spawning and abandons ♂. After three weeks the fry are released from the mouth.
Victorian Mouthbreeder *Haplochromis elegans*	39 inches (100 cm)	about 79°F (26°C) 5-15 dH, pH 7-8.5	Mother family. Aggressive. Egg spots.
Oreochromis mossambicus	59 inches (150 cm)	77-80.6°F (25-27°C) 8-20 dH, pH 7-7.5	Mother family. Very aggressive. ♂ mate in colonies. In spawning ♀ takes eggs in mouth and abandons ♂.
Black-chin Mouthbreeder *Sarotherodon melanotheron*	47 inches (120 cm)	75.2-82.4°F (24-28°C) 6-25 dH, pH 6.5-8	Father family. Sexual differences externally not recognizable. With some populations ♀ often also takes a few eggs into her mouth.

Breeding Instructions for Aquarium Fish

Reproduction and Rearing

Breeding takes place in the species tank.

Breeding tank. Not necessary,

Water. Raise the temperature to 77 to 82.4°F (25 to 28°C). Water composition as in the maintenance tank (see above).

Reproductive behavior. Larvophile mouthbreeders with mother family. The fish form pairs, but may be polygamous in very big aquariums with different species. The fish pick out a stone and clean it well. They then spawn like open breeders (see page 111). The female guards and tends the eggs, often at a distance of about 8 inches (20 cm). Occasionally she spits sand or small pebbles on the eggs (possibly for camouflage). When the young start to emerge, the female removes the sand and takes the larvae into her mouth. She helps them to emerge by sucking them out of the eggshells. After about seven days the mother disgorges the young from her mouth; however, she continues to care for and guide the fry for several weeks more.

Spawn. Up to 500 eggs.

Emergence of the young. At 78.8 to 82.4°F (26 to 28°C), after about 24 to 36 hours; a week after emerging the fry leave the mother's mouth.

Rearing. First food: microorganisms found in the basin, *Artemia* larvae, *Cyclops* larvae, fine ready-made rearing food.

Breeding data for Popular Cichlids: Larvophile Mouthbreeders

Name	Species Tank	Water Conditions	Comments ♂ = male, ♀ = female
Bujurquina vittata	39 inches (100 cm)	75.2-82.4°F (24-28°C) 5-15 dH, pH about 7	Parental family. Slightly aggressive. Spawn on stones or other foundation. After about 1½ days, both parents take the emerging larvae into their mouths. Partners exchange larvae with each other.
Chromidotilapia batesii	47 inches (120 cm)	77-80.6°F (25-27°C) 1-5 dH, pH 6.5	Father-mother family. Aggressive. Spawn in caves on cave roof. ♀ tends the spawn, ♂ defends territory. After emergence, ♀ takes larvae into mouth. Both parents guide free-swimming fry.
Satanoperca leuccosticta	47 inches (120 cm)	80.6-86°C (27-30°C) 4-18 dH, pH 6.5-7	Parental family. Aggressive. Spawn on stones. About 1½ days after spawning, both parents take eggs into mouth. Both parents guide free-swimming fry.

Breeding Instructions for Aquarium Fish

Labyrinth Fish
(Anabantoidei)

Labyrinth fish possess an accessory breathing organ—the labyrinth—which enables them to get air at the water surface. Young labyrinth fish at first breathe only through the gills. Their breathing labyrinth develops during the first weeks of life. The ability to breathe air increases the chances of survival of the fish in oxygen-poor, very warm water.

Reproductive Strategies of Labyrinth Fish

Labyrinth fish have developed different forms of brood care. There are mouthbreeders, hidden breeders, and those that build foam nests. In most species the males alone concern themselves with nest building and brood care (father family). There are also free-spawning species that do not care for their brood after spawning and even eat the eggs. Labyrinth fish can also be distinguished by their egg types. There are species with floating eggs and sinking eggs.

Floating eggs contain oil globules, and thus are lighter than water; after spawning, the eggs rise to the surface. The yolk sac of the hatched larvae still contains oil globules, so that the larvae float belly up on the surface. Labyrinth fish with floating eggs are open breeders or foam nest builders.

Sinking eggs contain no oil globules and are heavier than water. After spawning, they sink to the bottom. Labyrinth fish with sinking eggs are foam nest builders, mouthbreeders or cave breeders. The eggs are gathered up and taken into the mouth or carried into the foam nest. The larvae of foam nest builders are attached to the foam bubbles by means of sticky patches on their heads. If they fall, they are gathered by the father and spit back into the nest.

Asiatic Labyrinth Fish with Foam Nests and Floating Eggs

The paradise fish (*Macropodus opercularis*) is the best-known fish in this group. Other Asiatic labyrinth fish (see table below) are bred in the same manner.

Asiatic labyrinth fish with foam nests and floating eggs

Colisa sota, 1.9 inches (5 cm)
Giant gourami (*Colisa fasciata*), 3.9 inches (10 cm)
Thick-lipped gourami *(Colisa labiosa)*, 3.5 inches (9 cm)
Dwarf gourami (*Colisa lalia*), 1.9 inches (5 cm)
(see photos, pages 9 and 101)
Macropodus chinensis, 3.2 inches (8 cm)
Black paradise fish (*Macropodus concolor*), 4.7 inches (12 cm)
Paradise fish (*Macropodus opercularis*), 4.3 inches (11 cm)
Pearl gourami (*Trichogaster leeri*), 4.7 inches (12 cm)
(see illustration page 40).
Moonbeam gourami (*Trichogaster microlepis*), 5.9 inches (15 cm)
Blue gourami (*Trichogaster trichopterus*), 3.9 inches (10 cm)

Breeding Instructions for Aquarium Fish

Paradise fish
(*Macropodus opercularis*), 4.3 inches (15 cm)
Origin. Eastern Asia.
Habitat. Shallow, mostly stagnant waters (often rice fields).
Sexual differences. Males bigger and more splendid than the females, fin tips more elongated.
Maintenance tank. Species or community aquarium. Sexually mature males are very aggressive toward one another; do not put several together in one tank. Size: side lenth of 28 inches (70 cm) or more. Equipment: tank bed optional. Twigs, a few stones, dense border and background foliage (hardy species) as hiding places for the females, floating plants. Tank should be well-covered (fish leap).
Water. Temperature: 60.8 to 78.8°F (16 to 26°C). Hardness up to 30 dH is tolerated. pH: 6 to 8.
Food. Live and dry food of all kinds, not too small.

Reproduction and Rearing
The fish spawn regularly in the species or community aquarium. Take the females out after spawning, and put them into a special or community tank with the same water quality. After the brood care is over, take the male out also and raise the young in the species tank. As an alternative, place the fish pair in a breeding tank to spawn. After spawning, return the female to the maintenance tank (she can be pursued by the male in the breeding tank). The male cares for the eggs and repairs the nest until the fry swim independently. Then he too is returned to the maintenance tank.
Breeding tank. Same conditions as for the maintenance tank (see above). Remove the filter and ventilation if possible; a strong water current would damage the foam nest.
Water. Temperature: 77 to 86°F (25 to 30°C). Water composition like that of the maintenance tank (see above).
Reproductive behavior. Foam nest builders with floating eggs. The male alone builds the nest. He takes air from the surface into his mouth, mixes it with a secretion similar to sputum, and spits out the bubbles toward the surface. The bubbles rise to the surface and stick together in clumps. The male fastens his foam nest between or under floating plants or anchors it to a plant stem. He then woos the female with outspread fins and twisting motions. If the female is ready to spawn, she follows him under the nest. The male embraces her and turns her on her back. The male emits sperm, the female lays a few eggs, which float upward through the sperm cloud toward the nest. Then the male lets the female go, and the wooing starts anew.
Spawn. Up to 500 eggs.
Emergence of the young. After about 35 hours; three to four days later they leave the nest and swim on their own.
Rearing. First food: paramecia and rotifers; after about five or six days feed the fry with *Artemia* or *Cyclops* larvae, finely sifted pond food, and finely grated dry food. Rearing with grated dry food alone is possible, but the fish won't develop as well.

Breeding suggestion: When the fish spawn in the community aquarium, take the fry out after they swim independently and place them in a smaller rearing tank (same water as with a breeding tank). As an alternative, carefully slide the entire foam nest (before the fry are free-swimming) into a bowl, and place it in a rearing tank (same water as in the breeding tank).

Asiatic Labyrinth Fish with Foam Nests and Sinking Eggs

The best-known species in this group—and the most prolific spawner—is the Siamese fighting fish (*Betta splendens*). Other fighting fish are kept and bred in the same manner.

Asiatic labyrinth fish with foam nests and sinking eggs
Betta fasciata, 4.3 inches (11 cm)
Betta imbellis, 1.9 inches (4.8 cm)
Siamese fighting fish (*Betta splendens*), 2.8 inches (7 cm)

Siamese Fighting Fish

(**Betta splendens**) 2.8 inches (7 cm)
Origin. Southeast Asia. For the most part, only aquarium-bred forms (red, green, white, black, blue, and various color mixes) are available in stores.
Habitat. Stagnant and slowly flowing waters.
Sexual differences. Males are larger, more colorful, with much larger fins.
Maintenance tank. Species or community tank.
Caution. Adult males fight each other to death; therefore, never put two grown males in one tank. Size: side length of 12 inches (30 cm) or more. Equipment: tank bed optional. Fine-plumed foliage, roots, and plants as hiding places for females.
Water. Temperature: 77 to 82.4°F (25 to 28°C). Hardness to 25 dH. pH: 6 to 8. A water level of 8 inches (20 cm) is sufficient.
Food. Small live and dry food of all kinds.

Reproduction and Rearing

The fish spawn regularly in the maintenance tank. After spawning, take the females out and put them in a special or community tank with the same water composition. When the males stop tending the brood, take them out also, and rear the young in the species tank. Alternatively, transfer the young to a rearing tank of about 5 gallons (20 liters) with the same water composition as the maintenance tank. Or put the fish pair into a breeding tank and handle as above.
Breeding tank. Size and equipment the same as for the maintenance tank (see above). A tank of 1.3 to 2.6 gallons (5 to 10 liters) will do.
Water. Temperature: 82.4 to 86°F (28 to 30°C). Water composition same as for the maintenance tank (see above).
Reproductive behavior. Mating and spawning proceed as with the paradise fish (see page 127). The eggs, however, do not float up toward the nest but fall onto the anal fin of the male. After each spawning, the male gathers up the sinking eggs before they reach the ground; he carries them to the foam nest and spits them in. The male continues to build up the foam nest and tend the young until the fry are free-swimming.

Spawn. Includes 150 to 300 eggs.
Emergence of the young. After about 36 hours; three days later they leave the nest and swim on their own.
Rearing. The same as for paradise fish (see page 127).

Asiatic Labyrinth Fish: Mouthbreeding Fighting Fish

The best known mouthbreeder among the fighting fish is the mouthbreeding fighting fish (*Betta pugnax*). The other species (see table) are bred in the same manner.

Mouthbreeding fighting fish
Java fighting fish (*Betta picta*), 2.2 inches (5.5 cm)
Mouthbreeding fighting fish (*Beeta pugnax*), 3.9 inches (10 cm)
Banded fighting fish (*Betta taeniata*), 3.2 inches (8 cm)

Mouthbreeding Fighting Fish

(**Betta pugnax**), 3.9 inches (10 cm)
Origin. Southeast Asia.
Habitat. Running water and swift currents.
Sexual differences. Male more intensely colored, longer fins than female.
Maintenance tank. Species tank (the mouthbreeders are not as aggressive as the foam nest builders; several males can be kept together in one aquarium) or community aquarium with very calm fish. Size: side length of 24 inches (60 cm) or more. Equipment: tank bed optional. Fine-plumed plants, roots and stones as hiding places for females, water current (all mouthbreeding *Betta* species come from flowing waters).
Water. Temperature: 71.6 to 82.4°F (22 to 28°C). Hardness 6 to 12 dH. pH: 6 to 7.2.
Food. Live food of all kinds, suitable to the size of the fish; especially popular are black gnat larvae.

Breeding Instructions for Aquarium Fish

Reproduction and Rearing

Breeding occurs in the species tank (size, equipment and water same as for maintenance tank). Do not remove the brood-tending male after spawning. He would become strongly disturbed and would eat the eggs and the young ones. If he should be chased by the other tank occupants, the other fish must be carefully removed.

Reproductive behavior. Mouthbreeding care is an adaptation to life in swift-flowing waters, in which the building of foam nests is impossible. The head of mouthbreeders is larger than that of foam nest builders. Mouthbreeding labyrinth fish are territorial only during spawning. Mating is similar to that of foam nest builders, except the female usually is the more active partner. The male embraces the female just as with the foam nest builders, but he does not turn her over on her back. When the female has deposited some eggs, she slips out of the embrace, turns around, gathers the eggs from the anal fin of the male, and spits them into his mouth. The mating and spawning is repeated several times. The male keeps the eggs in his mouth until they hatch. After spawning, the female does not have to be removed from the tank.

Spawn. Can include over 100 eggs, but mostly fewer.

Emergence of the young. After about four days; four or five days later they consume the yolk sac and leave their father's mouth.

Rearing. The male doesn't take the young ones into his mouth again after he has left them; he can now be removed from the tank. First food: *Artemia* or *Cyclops* larvae.

Note. Unfortunately, the rearing of mouthbreeding *Betta* species succeeds only rarely. Most of the time the males eat the eggs or the emerged young on the third or fourth day.

Breeding suggestion: As soon as the young have left their father's mouth, they can be taken out and placed in a special rearing tank, about 5 gallons (20 liters) in volume, with the same water composition.

Asiatic Labyrinth Fish: Free Spawners

The only free-spawning Asiatic labyrinth fish that is regularly reared in the aquarium is the kissing gourami.

Kissing Gourami

(*Helostoma temmincki*), 5.9 inches (5 cm) (see photos, page 73).

These fish have greatly enlarged lips and an enormous disklike mouth with which they rasp away at algae on plants and rock. The fish press together their thick lips and "kiss" as a form of aggressive territorial display or mating ritual.

Origin. Thailand, Malaysia.

Habitat. Slowly flowing and stagnant waters.

Sexual differences. Uncertain.

Maintenance tank. Species or community aquarium. Size: side length of 47 inches (120 cm) for adult fish. Equipment: tank bed optional. Many tough plants (for example Java fern, *Anubias*); also floating plants.

Water. Temperature: 68 to 86°F (20 to 30°C). Hardness: 5 to 30 dH. pH: 6.8 to 8.5.

Food. Live and *d*ry food of all kinds, plants, algae, soaked lettuce, spinach (if the fish are accustomed to it). Delicate plants are eaten.

Reproduction and Rearing

The fish spawn regularly in the maintenance tank (species tank). After spawning remove the parents (egg eaters), or remove the eggs and transfer them to the rearing tank. Alternatively, place the fish pair in a breeding tank; after spawning, put both back into the maintenance tank.

Breeding tank. Same as the maintenance tank.

Water. Temperature: 77 to 86°F (25 to 30°C). Hardness: 5 to 10 dH. pH: 6.5 to 7.5.

Reproductive behavior. Mating is similar to that of other labyrinth fish; the female is the more active partner. The fish kiss each other on the mouth and the sides of the body. In spawning the male

embraces the female and lies under her. Spawning occurs mostly in the evening or at night.
Spawn. Large females can deposit up to 10,000 floating eggs. The eggs float upward and stick to plants.
Emergence of the young. At 78.8 to 82.4°F (26 to 28°C), after about 20 hours; three days later the fry swim on their own.
Rearing. First food: paramecia; after several days also fine dry food, *Artemia* larvae and finely sifted pond food.

African Labyrinth Fish:
Brood Tenders and Free Spawners

Labyrinth fish from Africa are cared for in the aquarium far more rarely than the Asiatic species. They belong predominantly to the genus *Ctenopoma*, which includes free spawners and foam nest builders. All have floating eggs. The species listed in the table have equal maintenance and breeding requirements.

Brood-tending African labyrinth fish
Ornate ctenopoma (*Ctenopoma ansorgii*)
3.2 inches (8 cm), West Africa
Ctenopoma nanum
3 inches (7.5 cm), West Africa

Origin. See table.
Habitat. Slowly flowing and stagnant water.
Sexual differences. Males larger; dorsal, tail, and anal fins more elongated than in females.
Maintenance tank. Species tank. Size: For small species from 24 inches (60 cm) for larger species from 39 inches (100 cm) side length. Equipment: tank bed optional. Roots as hiding places; dense foliage, but also large swimming area; floating plants for subduing the light. For large species powerful filtering, but not a very strong current.
Water. Temperature: 73.4 to 82.4°F (23 to 28°C). Hardness: 3 to 15 dH. pH: about 7.
Food. Live and dry food; live food suited to the size of the fish. For small species, insect larvae and small fish; for large species, rainworms and bigger fish; also thawed frozen food and food pellets.

Reproduction and Rearing
• Free spawners: Breeding in the species tank. Keep the fish in pairs; in very large aquariums keep several pairs or a male with several females. After spawning, take out the eggs and transfer them to a rearing tank.
• Brood tenders: Breeding in the species tank (keep fish in pairs). After spawning, take out females; after termination of the brood tending, take out the males also. Alternative 1: Take out free-swimming fry and transfer them to a rearing tank. Alternative 2: Bring the entire foam nest into the rearing tank shortly before the fry are free-swimming.
Rearing tank. Capacity: 5¼ gallons (20 liters) or more. Equipment: no tank bed or a thin layer of sand; fine plumed plants.
Water. Temperature. 77 to 86°F (25 to 30°C). Hardness: 3 to 8 dH. pH: about 6.5.
Reproductive behavior. Free spawners are not territorial and are more tolerant than the foam nest builders.
• In free spawners the male pursues the female relentlessly during courting. The male embraces the female during mating, which lasts a short time.
• In brood tenders the male builds a foam nest beneath and among the floating plants. Mating and spawning are similar to those in Asiatic labyrinth fish (see page 129).
Spawn. Different for each species; in smaller species; 50 to several hundred; in large free spawners up to 20,000 eggs.
Emergence of the young. At 82.4 to 86°F (28 to 30°C), after about 24 hours; two to three days later the fry swim on their own.
Rearing. First food: infusorians (paramecia, euglena); after about 1 week, *Artemia* larvae.

Breeding Instructions for Aquarium Fish

Fish Rarely Kept in Aquariums

Here is a group of fish that are rarely kept in the aquarium because of their bizarre appearance or special behavior. All of the fish can be bred in the aquarium at no great expense.

Butterfly fish
(Pantodon buchholzi)
Family *Pantodontidae*
Butterfly fish are sold in pet stores because of their strange appearance. The males are slimmer than the females, and their anal fins are sharply indented. Butterfly fish are difficult to breed because of their feeding habits (they eat only live food and only at or near the surface).

Malayan Half-beak
(Dermogenys pusillus)
Family *Hemirhamphidae*
Surface live-bearing fish that live only on insect food or on smaller fish. The newborn fry eat very fine powdered food. Insect food with vitamin supplements seems to be important for extended breeding without signs of degeneration. Vitamin E is especially important. *Dermogenys* can be bred with dry food alone over generations without problems if the food is saturated with plant oil containing vitamin E.

Syngnathus pulchellus
Family *Syngnathidae*
These fish are unsuited for community tanks. To begin spawning, they need small live food, consisting primarily of small crustaceans (for example Japanese water fleas). The eggs are delivered by the female into the "brood pouch" of the male, from which the larvae, 0.8 inches (2 cm) in length, emerge after three weeks. The fry are first nourished with rotifers and later with very small *Artemia* larvae.

Gobies
(for example, the Austrian Goby *Clamydogobius eremius*)
Family *Gobiidae*
Gobies are becoming more popular among aquarium hobbyists. Species that lay relatively large eggs can be bred easily. The males are more brighty colored than the females and own small territories with a cave in the center, in which spawning takes place. The fish can be bred in pairs in a tank with a capacity of 8 gallons (30 liters). The male alone cares for the brood until the emergence of the young. The hatched fry are transferred to a rearing tank and fed with *Artemia* larvae and dry rearing food. After three months they are a little over an inch (3 cm) long and sexually mature.

Puffers
(Tetraodon lorteti/Carinotetraodon somphongsi)
Family *Tetraodontidae*
Very comely, small species, not over $2^{1}/_{2}$ inches (6 cm) long, with beautiful mating coloring (red abdominal comb) in the males. The spawn of over 1500 eggs is guarded by the male until the fry, about 0.8 inches (2 cm) long, emerge. Rearing up to now has succeeded only with *Cyclops* larvae.

131

Breeding Instructions for Aquarium Fish

Spiny Eels

(for example, *Mastacembelus armatus*)
Family *Mastacembelidae*
After strenuous courting, the male mates with the egg-filled female. Both fish submerge themselves partially in the tank bed. The eggs should be gathered up and transferred to the rearing tank. After three to five days the young emerge and, after consuming the yolk sac, can be fed with *Artemia* larvae.

Bichirs

(for example, *Polypterus palmas* and *Polypterus ornatipinnis*)
Family *Polypteridae*
(see illustrations on page 14 and below)
Long-lived fish that need big aquariums. The sexes are differentiated by the size and shape of the anal fins. Spawning takes place after a stormy courtship. The male catches the eggs with his anal fin and fertilizes them. The eggs must be gathered up and transferred to a rearing tank. The larvae and fry still have outer gills, so that they look like salamander larvae.

Young bichirs look like salamanders. They possess tree-like outer gills.

Channa orientalis

Family *Channidae*
Interesting species remaining small (about 6 inches [5 cm]) of which there are two kinds, which show different behavior in brood care. One form, with abdominal fins, tends relatively many eggs in her mouth, and leads the fry to food. The other form, without abdominal fins, has fewer fry (which, however, after the incubation period in the mouth are better developed) and feeds these with unfertilized eggs. The fish are predators, and need nutrient-rich live food.

South American Knifefish

(for example, green knifefish, *Eigenmannia virescens*)
Order *Gymnotiformes*
The green knifefish can be kept in a large tank (about 79 gallons [300 liters]) in a small breeding colony. The large male controls the female and woos with weak electrical signals, which also serve as orientation. The fish must be brought to spawning by imitating the rainy seasons, after the Kirschbaum method (see page 66). Rearing of the fry succeeds with *Artemia* larvae.

Elephant Fish

(for example, *Pollimyrus isidori*)
Classification *Mormyriformes*
This fish must also be induced to spawn by the method described on page 66. Males build up territories, which they defend extremely aggressively. In the center of the territory they build a globe-shaped nest out of fine-plumped plants, into which the eggs are laid. Like the parents, the larvae have weak electric organs.

Literature and Addresses

Books

Braemer, Helga and Ines Scheurmann: *Tropical Fish* (Barron's, 1983).

Hansen, J.: *Making Your Own Aquarium* (Bell and Hyman, 1979).

Hawkins, A. D. (Editor): *Aquarium Systems* (Academic Press, 1981).

Hellner, Steffen: *Killifish* (Barron's, 1990).

Pinter, Helmut: *Labyrinth Fish* (Barron's, 1986).

Ramshorst, J. D. van (Editor): *The Complete Aquarium Encyclopedia* (Phaidon, 1978).

Scheurmann, Ines: *The New Aquarium Handbook* (Barron's, 1986).

————: *Water Plants in the Aquarium* (Barron's, 1987).

Sterba, G.: *The Aquarists' Encyclopedia* (Blandford, 1983).

Ward, Brian: *Aquarium Fish Survival Manual* (Barron's, 1985).

Magazines

Aquarium Fish Magazine
P.O. Box 6050
Mission Viejo, CA 92690

Freshwater and Marine Aquarium
144 West Sierra Madre Boulevard
Sierra Madre, CA 91024

Practical Fishkeeping Magazine
RR1, Box 200 D
Jonesburg, MO 63351

Tropical Fish Hobbyist
One TFH Plaza
Third and Union Avenues
Neptune City, NJ 07753

Specialty Societies

American Cichlid Association
P.O. Box 32130
Raleigh, NC 27622

American Killifish Association
903 Merrifield Place
Mishawaka, IN 46544

American Livebearer Association
50 N. Second St.
St. Clair, PA 17970

British Cichlid Association
33 Kirkmeadow,
Bretton,
Peterborough. PE3 8JG
England

British Discus Association
P.O. Box 9168
Canton, OH 44711-9168
or
41 Pengwern,
Llangollen,
Clwyd. LL20 8AT
England

Catfish Association of North America
Box 45
Rt. 104A
Sterling, NY 13156

International Fancy Guppy Association
2312 Pestalozzi,
St. Louis, MO 63118

North American Discus Society
P.O. Box 5145
Lakeland, FL 33807

North American Fish Breeders Guild
4731 Lake Avenue
Rochester, NY 14612

Index

Index

Index

Index

Index

Perfect for Pet Owners!

PET OWNER'S MANUALS

Over 50 illustrations per book
(20 or more color photos),
72-80 pp., paperback.

AFRICAN GRAY PARROTS (3773-1)
AMAZON PARROTS (4035-X)
BANTAMS (3687-5)
BEAGLES (3829-0)
BEEKEEPING (4089-9)
BOXERS (4036-8)
CANARIES (4611-0)
CATS (4442-1)
CHINCHILLAS (4037-6)
CHOW-CHOWS (3952-1)
CICHLIDS (4597-1)
COCKATIELS (4610-2)
COCKATOOS (4159-3)
CONURES (4880-6)
DACHSHUNDS (2888-0)
DALMATIANS (4605-6)
DISCUS FISH (4669-2)
DOBERMAN PINSCHERS (2999-2)
DOGS (4822-9)
DWARF RABBITS (1352-2)
FEEDING AND SHELTERING
   BACKYARD BIRDS (4252-2)
FEEDING AND SHELTERING
   EUROPEAN BIRDS (2858-9)
FERRETS (2976-3)
GERBILS (3725-1)
GERMAN SHEPHERDS (2982-8)
GOLDEN RETRIEVERS (3793-6)
GOLDFISH (2975-5)
GOULDIAN FINCHES (4523-8)
GUINEA PIGS (4612-9)
HAMSTERS (4439-8)
IRISH SETTERS (4663-3)
KILLIFISH (4475-4)
LABRADOR RETRIEVERS (3792-8)
LHASA APSOS (3950-5)
LIZARDS IN THE TERRARIUM (3925-4)
LONGHAIRED CATS (2803-1)
LONG-TAILED PARAKEETS (1351-4)
LOVEBIRDS (3726-X)
MACAWS (4768-0)
MICE (2921-6)
MINIATURE PIGS (1356-5)
MUTTS (4126-7)
MYNAHS (3688-3)
PARAKEETS (4437-1)
PARROTS (4823-7)

PERSIAN CATS (4405-3)
PIGEONS (4044-9)
POMERANIANS (4670-6)
PONIES (2856-2)
POODLES (2812-0)
RABBITS (4440-1)
RATS (4535-1)
ROTTWEILERS (4483-5)
SCHNAUZERS (3949-1)
SHAR-PEI (4834-2)
SHEEP (4091-0)
SHETLAND SHEEPDOGS (4264-6)
SHIH TZUS (4524-6)
SIAMESE CATS (4764-8)
SIBERIAN HUSKIES (4265-4)
SNAKES (2813-9)
SPANIELS (2424-9)
TROPICAL FISH (4700-1)
TURTLES (4702-8)
YORKSHIRE TERRIERS (4406-1)
ZEBRA FINCHES (3497-X)

NEW PET HANDBOOKS

Detailed, illustrated profiles (40-60
color photos), 144 pp., paperback.

NEW AQUARIUM FISH HANDBOOK
   (3682-4)
NEW AUSTRALIAN PARAKEET
   HANDBOOK (4739-7)
NEW BIRD HANDBOOK (4157-7)
NEW CANARY HANDBOOK (4879-2)
NEW CAT HANDBOOK (2922-4)
NEW COCKATIEL HANDBOOK (4201-8)
NEW DOG HANDBOOK (2857-0)
NEW DUCK HANDBOOK (4088-0)
NEW FINCH HANDBOOK (2859-7)
NEW GOAT HANDBOOK (4090-2)
NEW PARAKEET HANDBOOK (2985-2)
NEW PARROT HANDBOOK (3729-4)
NEW RABBIT HANDBOOK (4202-6)
NEW SALTWATER AQUARIUM
   HANDBOOK (4482-7)
NEW SOFTBILL HANDBOOK (4075-9)
NEW TERRIER HANDBOOK (3951-3)

FIRST AID FOR PETS

Fully illustrated, colorful guide, 20 pp.,
Hardboard with hanging chain and
   index tabs.

FIRST AID FOR YOUR CAT (5827-5)
FIRST AID FOR YOUR DOG (5828-3)

REFERENCE BOOKS

Comprehensive, lavishly illustrated
references (60-300 color photos),
136-176 pp., hardcover & paperback
AQUARIUM FISH (1350-6)
AQUARIUM FISH BREEDING
   (4474-6), paperback
AQUARIUM FISH SURVIVAL
   MANUAL (5686-8), hardcover
BEST PET NAME BOOK EVER, THE
   (4258-1), paperback
CAT CARE MANUAL (5765-1),
   hardcover
CIVILIZING YOUR PUPPY (4953-5)
COMMUNICATING WITH YOUR
   DOG (4203-4), paperback
COMPLETE BOOK OF
   BUDGERIGARS (6059-8),
   hardcover
COMPLETE BOOK OF CAT CARE,
   Paperback (4613-7)
COMPLETE BOOK OF DOG CARE,
   Paperback (4158-5)
COMPLETE BOOK OF PARROTS
   (5971-9), hardcover
DOG CARE MANUAL (5764-3),
   hardcover
GOLDFISH AND ORNAMENTAL
   CARP (5634-5), hardcover
GUIDE TO HOME PET GROOMING
   (4298-0), paperback
HOP TO IT: A Guide to
   Training Your Pet Rabbit
   (4551-3), paperback
HORSE CARE MANUAL (5795-3),
   hardcover
HOW TO TEACH YOUR OLD DOG
   NEW TRICKS (4544-0),
   paperback
LABYRINTH FISH (5635-3),
   hardcover
MACAWS (6073-3), hardcover
NONVENOMOUS SNAKES (5632-9),
   hardcover
WATER PLANTS IN THE AQUARIUM
   (3926-2), paperback

Barron's Educational Series, Inc. • 250 Wireless Blvd., Hauppauge, NY 11788
Call toll-free: 1-800-645-3476 • In Canada: Georgetown Book Warehouse
34 Armstrong Ave., Georgetown, Ont. L7G 4R9 • Call toll-free: 1-800-247-7160
ISBN prefix: 0-8120 • Order from your favorite book or pet store

BARRON'S

BARRON'S PREMIUM PET CARE SERIES

- One-volume, all-inclusive hardcover & paperback reference books
- Illustrated with from 80 to 300 stunning full-color photos, plus numerous drawings and charts.

AQUARIUM FISH SURVIVAL MANUAL, THE by Ward. A directory of more than 300 marine and freshwater fish species, including a guide to aquatic plants. 176 pp., 7³/₄" x 10", $19.95 NCR (5686-8) Hardcover.

AUSTRALIAN FINCHES: THE COMPLETE BOOK OF by Mobbs. An A-to-Z encyclopedia styled book, listing various finch species, cages, aviaries, flights, breeding etc. 144 pp., 8" x 11¹/₄", $18.95, NCR (6091-1) Hardcover.

BEST PET NAME BOOK EVER, THE by Eldridge. Presents 22 lists of names — 1500 in all to help give a pet the best name ever. 208 pp., 6¹⁵/₁₆" x 6¹⁵/₁₆", $5.95, Can. $7.95, (4258-1) Paperback.

THE COMPLETE BOOK OF BUDGERIGARS by B. Moizer & S. Moizer. The definitive reference on one of the world's most popular pets—Budgerigars (e.g. Parakeets). 144 pp., 8" x 11¹/₄", $16.95, NCR (6059-8) Hardcover.

THE CAT CARE MANUAL by Viner. Shows you how to meet all the needs of your cat and helps you understand its behavior. 160 pp., 7⁵/₈" x 9¹³/₁₆", $16.95, Can. $22.95 (5765-1) Hardcover.

COMMUNICATING WITH YOUR DOG by Baer. How to train your dog intelligently and humanely. 144 pp., 6¹/₂" x 7⁷/₈" (4203-4) $8.95, Can. $11.95 Paperback.

COMPLETE BOOK OF DOG CARE, THE by Klever. Dog-care expert answers questions about selecting, training, grooming and health care. 176 pp., 6⁵/₈" x 9¹/₄", $8.95, Can. $11.95 (4158-5) Paperback.

THE DOG CARE MANUAL by Alderton. Gives you expert pointers on the general and medical care of your dog, as well as on obedience training. 160 pp., 7⁵/₈" x 9¹³/₁₆", $16.95, Can. $22.95 (5764-3) Hardcover.

GOLDFISH AND ORNAMENTAL CARP by Penzes & Tölg. Covers everything from anatomy, biology and varieties to nutrition, "housing," and diseases. 136 pp., 7³/₄" x 10", $18.95, Can. $25.95 (5634-5) Hardcover.

THE HORSE CARE MANUAL by May. A veterinary surgeon covers all facets of horse and pony ownership, through a convenient question-and-answer format. 160 pp., 7¹/₂" x 9³/₄", $16.95, NCR (5795-3) Hardcover.

LABYRINTH FISH by Pinter. Teaches you about the feeding, breeding, and diseases of these fish, and about aquarium maintenance. 136 pp., 7³/₄" x 10", $18.95, Can. $25.95 (5635-3) Hardcover.

NONVENOMOUS SNAKES by Trutnau. Features detailed descriptions of over 100 snake species and covers feeding, breeding, illnesses, and terrariums. 192 pp., 7³/₄" x 10", $18.95, Can. $25.95 (5632-9) Hardcover.

THE COMPLETE BOOK OF PARROTS by Low. Everything that anyone needs to know about owning all kinds of parrots, as well as macaws, cockatoos, parakeets, and lories. 144 pp., 7⁷/₈" x 11", $16.95, NCR (5971-9) Hardcover.

WATER PLANTS IN THE AQUARIUM by Scheurmann. Professional guidance in choosing the most suitable water plants for various types of aquariums and fish. 72 pp., 6¹/₂" x 7⁷/₈", $4.50, Can. $5.95 (3926-2) Paperback.

ISBN Prefix: 0-8120
Barron's Educational Series, Inc.
250 Wireless Boulevard, Hauppauge, New York 11788, For instant service call toll-free: 1-800-645-3476 In N. Y. call 1-800-257-5729.
In Canada: Georgetown Book Warehouse, 34 Armstrong Avenue, Georgetown, Ontario L7G 4R9. Sales: (416) 458-5506

Books can be purchased at your bookstore or directly from Barron's. Enclose check or money order for total amount plus sales tax where applicable and 10% for postage (minimum charge $1.50, Can. $2.00). All major credit cards are accepted. Prices subject to change without notice.